FUNERAL FRAMES

STORIES TO CAPTURE A LIFE WELL LIVED

RICHARD E. ZAJAC

CSS Publishing Company, Inc.

Lima, Ohio

FUNERAL FRAME

FIRST EDITION
Copyright © 2021
by CSS Publishing Co., Inc.

Library of Congress Cataloging-in-Publication Data

Names: Zajac, Richard E., 1949- author.
Title: Funeral frames : stories to capture a life well lived / Richard E.
   Zajac.
Description: First edition. | Lima, Ohio : CSS Publishing Company, Inc.,
   2022. | Includes index.
Identifiers: LCCN 2021061156 (print) | LCCN 2021061157 (ebook) | ISBN
   9780788030703 | ISBN 9780788030710 (ebook)
Subjects: LCSH: Bereavement--Religious aspects--Christianity--Anecdotes. |
   Grief--Religious aspects--Christianity--Anecdotes. | Death--Religious
   aspects--Christianity--Anecdotes. | Consolation.
Classification: LCC BV4905.3 .Z35 2022 (print) | LCC BV4905.3 (ebook) |
   DDC 248.8/6--dc23/eng/20220118
LC record available at https://lccn.loc.gov/2021061156
LC ebook record available at https://lccn.loc.gov/2021061157

For more information about CSS Publishing Company resources, visit our website at www.csspub.com, email us at csr@csspub.com, or call (800) 241-4056.

e-book:
ISBN-13: 978-0-7880-3071-0
ISBN-10: 0-7880-3071-x

ISBN-13: 978-0-7880-3070-3
ISBN-10: 0-7880-3070-1   DIGITALLY
PRINTED

CONTENTS

INTRODUCTION

When I was a young curate, I discovered quickly the challenge, the dread, the heartache and the pain that came when called upon to preach at a funeral, a call that came quite frequently. The liturgical instructions called for the homily to stress the promise of the resurrection, the award awaiting a righteous life, and all the faith components that come with death. A eulogy was discouraged and actually frowned upon. As I saw it, those instructions made the preacher's task relatively simple. There was no need to sit down with the family and learn vital details of their loved one's life, no need to spend time at the wake asking visitors their impression of the person who had died. No need to agonize the night before the funeral so as to properly pay tribute to the deceased individual's life. That person's life was to be but a footnote in one's overall homily.

That never set well with me. We do a disservice to a life well lived, a life worthy of respect and admiration and affection when their name barely gets mentioned amidst a summary of our beliefs in a life hereafter, a summary which many in the congregation may have heard many times over, a summary that's applicable to anyone regardless of the life they lived. And it seems to me that it's a bit unfair and somewhat disingenuous that we can eulogize a priest on the day of their funeral, but not eulogize a member of the rank-and-file of our church, who far outnumber and sometimes even better serve the people of God than those of clergy status. Furthermore, with more and more churches disallowing a eulogy via friend or member of the deceased's family, there's the travesty of a life well lived and well loved being celebrated with little, if any, distinction.

Most surely, there will be many we are called upon to bury whose lives were nondescript; whose life may well have had an overwhelming number of negative characteristics. The eulogy would then, of course, give way to references to the Paschal Candle, the funeral pall, metaphors regarding butterflies and changing seasons, and other varied ways to highlight the promise of the resurrection.

As difficult and as painstaking as the composition of a eulogy may be, I believe we owe it to the one we've been given the task to bury. I believe it's a high crime when the homily we would preach at Nelson Mandela's funeral bears little difference to the one we would preach at John Gotti's funeral.

I liken this book to that portfolio the mythical Mr. Phelps would open after hearing that tape that would self destruct after he listened to it, that tape that outlined his "Mission Impossible" on that fabled television show which bore that name. You'll recall how Mr. Phelps would sift through that portfolio, looking at the pictures of potential candidates to carry out his mission, candidates who possessed the skill set necessary to accomplish the task at hand. I see the stories that follow as a portfolio of possible lead ups to best capture the particular gifts and talents and character traits that marked the life of the person we need to eulogize.

I realize that it's often an impossible mission to not only find the time to meet with the family of the deceased, but also to find the time to make it to a crowded wake to secure additional information about the person we're burying. And that, of course, is in addition to burning the midnight oil so we might compose a fitting tribute to the one whose funeral we have been honored to conduct. And we are talking in some cases of clergy who are the Pastors of an aging congregation, where the funerals are many.

This book is one that I wish I would've had at the beginning of my priestly ministry and one that may be especially helpful to priests and ministers and deacons and rabbis whose funeral load may well be more than he or she can bear. It may well be difficult not to repeat certain funeral illustrations, but this wide variety of illustrations may help broaden the breadth of a pastor's funeral repertoire and keep congregations from shaking their heads at the boilerplate homily that they might've heard ten times over.

At the beginning of each chapter is a brief instruction of how the story or illustration which immediately follows might be used in your homily. I then follow that with an example of how I used that illustration to eulogize the life of someone at whose funeral I had been asked to preside. I hope you'll find what I've done helpful in your application of that "frame" if it's the one you'll choose to "capture a well lived life."

The closing illustrations are meant to stand alone, but may well be used to underline an aspect of the deceased's life that should be underlined or which hadn't been mentioned earlier in the eulogy. I've interchanged the fictitious John and Mary Smith to personalize the story.

OPENING STORIES

IF YOU BUILD IT, THEY WILL COME

You need to describe the wonderful experiences of that person's life and tell of the wonderful memories they've left behind.

There was a movie made several years back that I believe many will remember. The movie starred Kevin Costner. It was entitled *A Field of Dreams*. It's a beautiful, whimsical tale of a young farmer who hears a voice from a cornfield say: "If you build it, they will come!"[1] "Build what?" He wants to know. Build a baseball diamond was the answer. "Who will come?" He wants to know. He learns that it would be Shoeless Joe Jackson and other late and great stars of the Chicago White Sox.

The farmer plows under a huge part of that cornfield and builds a ball diamond complete with viewing stands and lights. After a few short days, Shoeless Joe Jackson walks in from the cornfield and so do eight other members of the fabled Chicago White Sox. They are joined by members of the New York Giants as well as the farmer's dad, who was a ballplayer with some unfinished business to attend to with his son. They begin playing baseball and eventually an endless line of cars can be seen streaming towards the ballpark to fill its seats and view the games they longed to see.

It's a warm and tender story and it sounds crazy if you haven't seen it, but I believe it captures in a metaphorical way the life of John Buerk. Many years ago, John Buerk heard a voice say: "If you build it, they will come!" But in John's case, it wasn't the building of a ball diamond that would be his charge; it was the building of a beautiful and a marvelous life. And what will come would be wonderful experiences and great memories. John Buerk built a beautiful and marvelous life and wonderful experiences, and great memories did indeed come.

There was first of all the wonderful experience of being married to Jill. I never heard the details of how they met, but if

---

1 Field of Dreams, directed by Phil Alden Robinson (1989; New York, Universal Pictures Home Entertainment, 2009).

there were ever two people made for each other, it was John and Jill. They both shared a love for music, they both had an eye for beautiful things, they both loved the arts and loved the classics and loved to teach and loved engaging conversations. And as much as John always had an eye for a pretty woman, none could compare with Jill. John adored her.

And then how about the family the two of them created: Dietrich, Linda, and Christian. They were the purveyors of tremendous joy and pride for the two of them, and they provided them with many wonderful experiences.

Of course, there are the grandchildren. Thank God, John got to see and hold his latest grandchild a few weeks before he died. Those grandkids lit up John's life especially in his retirement years. They, too, were purveyors of tremendous joy and pride. They, too, provided John and Jill with many wonderful experiences.

And then how about John's years as a Lutheran Pastor? His pastoral skills were responsible for the building up of this church (Parkside Lutheran), a church that had a marvelously eclectic congregation, a church that had the finest of music, the most extraordinary of sermons, and the most uplifting of liturgies. Many wonderful things were happening here on a regular basis thanks to John. And that not only did John proud, but it provided him with many wonderful experiences.

And there were also his years at the University of Buffalo, first as a campus minister, then as an administrator, and then as a faculty member. John's brilliant mind, his knowledge of a vast array of subjects, his down to earth touch when it came to the courses he taught and the complicated issues he'd discuss, made him a popular figure on the UB campus. And over those years John was provided with wonderful experiences of conversations and relationships that thoroughly enriched his life.

And then there was John's involvement in ecumenical and interfaith affairs which would lead to his appointment as the ecumenical officer not only of the Lutheran Church here in Buffalo, but of the entire Synod. And there would also be John's involvement in many community organizations, serving on their boards and participating in their activities. Those organizations not only enriched his life beyond measure but also enriched the lives of the many people with whom he interacted and with whom, on more than a few occasions, would share a drink or two or three.

And there were also his record-setting appearances at the pulpit of the renowned Holloway Chapel in Pt. Abino, Canada. You couldn't find a better preacher than John Buerk. And then there's his beloved Chautauqua Institution. If there was ever a definition for a Chautauquan, John fit the bill. Throughout his life, John had many experiences and encounters which ultimately provided him with a rich and wonderful life.

So, all in all, in the many roles John assumed in the course of his life, I believe it can well be said that there is plenty of evidence that multiple wonderful experiences came out of the cornfields of the places where John lived and worked, and all of them became compliments of the marvelous and beautiful life which John Buerk happened to build.

And also, from that marvelous and beautiful life that John had built, there came, for you and me and thousands of others, there came many great memories.

There's first of all the memory of all those jokes John liked to tell. Anytime I called John, before we got to what I was calling about, John would say to me: "Did you hear that one about…" And, as many of you know, many of those jokes could not be repeated at this pulpit.

And there was also for you and me and others the memory of John's charm. He always had a twinkle in his eye, a smile on his face, and he was one of those guys it was hard not to like. Then there's the memory of John's wit, how he knew just the right thing to say, and how to say it. And John, of course, not only had a great wit, but he was absolutely brilliant when it came to so many things which made him a welcomed guest at the homes of some of the sharpest minds in Western New York. Is it any wonder how John got the renowned and brilliant and famous Krister Stendhal to come to his house? Their conversation was so enthralling that it needed to continue with, of course, a spot or two or three of cognac.

And also, for you and I and others, there's the memory of John as a great listener. I saw Dr. Jim Paul, John's physician, just the other day and he shared with me a story John told of how, when he was a theological student in Germany, his roommate was having a breakdown and all he spoke was German and the only German that John knew were the words "Ich verstehe" which translated means "I understand." Although John didn't understand a word of what that German roommate was telling him, John would say on occasion "Ich verstehe." And that proved to be all that was needed because John's listening skills would serve to ultimately quell the man's breakdown. Those listening skills would make John a great and sought-after counselor who would ease the pain of many and be always remembered by many for the help he provided them.

And you and I and so many others have the great memory of John as always upbeat, always affable, always positive, someone who could light up any room he walked into and put a damper upon any gloom and doom that might've been in evidence.

And there's also the memory of John as a scholar, a lifelong learner, who would thirst for new knowledge and new insights and better ways of ministry. And along with that came John's support of women in ministry and his advocacy for social justice. Just as John fit the bill when it came to the definition of a Chautauquan, he also fit the bill when it came to the definition a Renaissance Man.

There is also a great memory of John as a seed planter. Roger Griffiths III told me how John took him out to lunch one day and said: "Roger, did you ever think about becoming a Lutheran Minister?" And Roger said that lunch was responsible for his vocation. And John didn't just do that for Roger, but he did that for a lot of other people, not necessarily asking them to consider priesthood, but asking them to do something with their skills to better the church, the community, or even themselves.

And also, how can we forget how John was a master "disarmer". No matter what might be our beef or what might be troubling us or what might be angering us, you would melt in John's presence. And when he gave you a hug, you'd feel his heart touching yours.

And of course, it goes without saying that there will always be our remembrance of John as an imbiber of fine cognac and fine single malt scotch, but also cheap beer. Never putting on airs, John could dialogue with the janitor as well as the university president and he was loved by all.

All in all, John Buerk's life, in a metaphorical way, followed the script of the movie *A Field of Dreams*. When John was very young, he heard God tell him: "If you build it, they will come." John built the beautiful and marvelous life God called him to build and from the cornfields of the places where John had lived and worked, there came for John wonderful experiences and there came for us a great many wonderful memories. And I'm sure God was mighty proud of what John had built with the gifts that God had given him.

We're here today not just to pay tribute to John's life, but to pay tribute to our faith, a faith that tells us that although the body of John Buerk lies in death, he's gained an everlasting dwelling place in heaven. A faith that tells us that when we die, life is changed not ended.

John is living now in God's celestial kingdom where peace and happiness eternally reigns. And can you imagine the fun he's having meeting up with those he loved and lost in life? Can you imagine all the jokes John's already told them?

THE RIVER BOAT

Tell of their valiant struggle and the virtues they embodied despite the demon they could not conquer.

Two strangers, a small boy and an older man, were fishing from the banks of the Mississippi River. As time passed, they discovered that, although the fishing was poor, the conversation was good. By the time the sun began to set, they had talked of many things. At dusk, a large riverboat was seen moving slowly in the distance. When the boy saw the boat, he began to shout and wave his arms that he might attract the attention of those on board. The older man watched for some time and said: "Son, you're foolish if you think that boat is going to stop for you. It's on its way to some unknown place and it surely won't stop for a young boy." Suddenly, the boat began to slow and veer toward the riverbank. To the older man's amazement, the boat came near enough to shore that a gangplank could be lowered upon the land. The boy ran up the plank and entered the boat and then, turning to his new friend on the shore, he said: "I'm not foolish, mister! You see, my father is the captain of this boat, and we're going to a new home up the river."

My fellow grievers, this past Friday, the ship of death made an unexpected stop along the river of life and picked up our friend Jim. The good news is that God was the captain of that ship, and that ship has made its way to Jim's new home, where peace and happiness eternally reigns.

Unfortunately for Jim, peace and happiness was not something he was able to secure very well in this life. When John lost his dad at 13 years of age, he grieved terribly. He had lost his best friend and, from that day on, there was a hole in his heart that never did get filled.

And then when adolescence passed, the demon of alcohol took hold of his life, and it was a demon that Jim could never really shake. Jim found solace in helping those he loved. When Jessica needed help, when she needed to be bailed out of a problem that had consumed her life, Jim was there for her. And when Carol made the big move to West Virginia, Jim was there to help with the move and, upon arrival, he painted the house next door so Carol wouldn't have to look at ugliness when she awoke in the morning. For the nuns who lived on the property near Carol's home, Jim became their handyman. If there was grass that needed cutting, Jim would do it. If there was something that needed fixing, Jim would fix it. And that was true not just for those nuns, but it was true for anyone in need.

Jim's passion rested in race cars. He loved NASCAR and he loved his two Pontiac Firebirds which he tinkered with on an almost daily basis.

Jim left us much too early, but I believe that the hole in his heart is now filled and he's back with his dad again, and the demon of alcohol has finally been conquered. He is now sober, happy, full and at peace, enjoying all the benefits of God's celestial kingdom, which Jesus promised.

MILLION DOLLAR SMILE

Tell of the varied ways their smile impacted not only their life, but the lives of those they loved.

They conducted an interesting study some years ago as to the impact of our appearance upon the paycheck we happen to receive. They analyzed the employment data of seven thousand adults, and they came to the conclusion that those who were above average in appearance earned far more than those who were below average in appearance. And although appearance has to do with the shine on our shoes, the crease in our clothing, or our personal grooming habits; the research study found that the number one part of our appearance, the biggest factor when it came to a higher paycheck had to do with our face and, in particular, whether or not it wore a smile.

The Parker Pen Company published a guide to international behavior entitled *The Do's and Taboos from Around the World* and it lists all the things we need to be careful about when traveling abroad. In the postscript on the last page, it tells of the one universal action, the one signal, the one form of communication that is used and understood by every culture and in every country and that happens to be the smile.[2]

A Dr. Paul Erkin did research on more than two hundred different kinds of smiles and came to the conclusion that a person can alter their immune efficiency by putting a smile upon their face; that when people smile, there's an increased blood flow to the brain, resulting in the release of neuro chemicals responsible for health and healing.

The employment manager of a large New York department store reported that she would rather hire a salesclerk of limited

2Parker Pen Company, Do's and Taboos Around The World, edited by Roger Axtell (Hoboken, NJ: Wiley, 1993).

21

education who wore a smile than hire a Doctor of Philosophy that wore a somber face.

In hospitals, patients felt that a smiling nurse helped them to heal more quickly, and waiters and waitresses have reported making bigger tips when they wore a smile.

I've been relating to you the benefits and perks of a smile because Nancy Campbell had a million-dollar smile, Nancy's smile could light up a room; Nancy's smile was her trademark and her calling card. And despite a horrendous illness that kept her bedridden for several months at Sisters Hospital, despite having little to smile about over these past several months, whenever myself or one of the nurses would visit her, she still flashed that smile. A smile would be something that would occupy her face the minute she saw yours.

And even if Nancy had never cashed in on those benefits and perks of a smile which I had talked about earlier, it can be said that she's cashing in on them now because from this day forward, when someone flashes a smile at us, we're going to remember Nancy. From this day forward, when someone flashes a smile at us, were going to smile as well, because in remembering Nancy, we're going to remember many wonderful things.

We are going to remember as to what a great wife she happened to be. Details are a little sketchy, but the word was that when her husband Tom first met her, he fell in love with her and then used his power as a State Trooper to find ways to see her. The two of them were married for fifty-five years.

In remembering Nancy, we're going to remember as to what a great mom she happened to be. Be it Sherry or be it her son Tom with whom she's now sharing eternal life, she taught them not only right from wrong, but she taught them the value of family and the importance of nurturing relationships. The Campbell home was ground zero for family activity. The backyard pool was a staple for summertime fun and, you name the holiday, you could always count on a large family gathering at the Campbell home.

In remembering Nancy Campbell, the grandkids are going to remember that they had one of the greatest grandmothers that money could buy. They were the apples of Nancy's eyes, and they knew it. And nothing pleased her more than caring for them, babysitting them, loving them.

In remembering Nancy Campbell, the nieces and nephews and friends and all of us here are going to remember what a beautiful woman she happened to be, not just in appearance but in the way she conducted her life. We'll remember her garden and how much she loved working that garden. We'll remember what a great animal lover she happened to be, what a social butterfly she was; and we'll remember how she could always be counted on for a kindness, for sympathy or for loving care. In recalling Nancy Campbell, we're going to remember her valiant fight against her illness, a fight which unfortunately she could not win. In remembering Nancy Campbell's life, we're going to have a lot to smile about because it was a life well lived and well loved and there will be an abundance of memories which upon recall, we can't help but smile.

David Brooks wrote a book some time ago that was entitled: *The Road to Character*. In it, he made a point about resume virtues and eulogy virtues and how too many of us chase after resume virtues (accomplishments, achievements, awards) and not enough chase after eulogy virtues (character, kindness, excellence, integrity).[3] Nancy Campbell had her share of resume virtues, but what made her a standout in life was her abundance of eulogy virtues; her kindness, her integrity, her willingness to give of herself, to name a few. Nancy has left behind a wonderful legacy.

Just a few short days from now, we will celebrate Easter; we will celebrate the fact of Jesus' death on the cross as not being the end of his life. We will be celebrating Jesus' rising from the dead and the promise that went with it: the promise that when we die, we will rise as well, that our life doesn't end with our death, that it continues on.

So, when someone flashes a smile at us, we will smile as well because we'll remember Nancy Campbell and we'll smile about the fact that she lives in God's celestial kingdom where peace and happiness eternally reigns.

3 David Brooks, The Road to Character (New York: Random House, 2015), XI.

Some of you might recall a clown character played by Emmitt Kelly. The character was called Weary Willie. He was a sad looking fellow who never spoke and never cracked a smile. His act was to juggle three balls while balancing a peacock feather on his nose and, when he dropped one of the balls, he'd bend over to pick it up. The crowd would roar with laughter because the feather never left his nose. It had been stuck into a hidden piece of putty on the tip of his nose.

My friends, if you want to pay tribute to Nancy Campbell, don't be a Weary Willie or a Weary Willa. Turn your frowns into smiles and think of Nancy when you do.

NAME ON A TOMBSTONE

Tell of what comes to mind when you hear or see their name and then describe the indelible mark they left upon the souls of those who benefited by their presence.

Some years ago, I had the opportunity to make a trip to Washington and I had a chance to visit the Vietnam Memorial Wall. As many of you know, it's a long black granite wall with thousands of names of those who lost their lives in that tragic conflict. As I walked the grounds of the Wall, I couldn't help but notice the silence, the sense of reverence resonating everywhere. I also couldn't help but notice how, when people found the name of a loved one, they'd rub their fingers across the name, many doing so with tears running down their face. You could tell from the tears that what they rubbed was more than a name on that wall, there was a person behind the name, a person who was loved and cherished and horribly missed, a person who was with them for far too brief a time but in that time left an indelible mark upon their soul.

For many people, Tessie Gornikiewicz will be but a name in the obituary column of the local newspaper. For many who will visit Hillcrest cemetery, Tessie Gornikiewicz will be a name on a mausoleum wall. But to all of us present today, Tessie Gornikiewicz is more than just a name. And if we were to rub our fingers across that name, it would conjure up all sorts of memories; it would bring to mind all the indelible marks Tessie left upon our souls.

There would be the memory and the mark of someone who exuded compassion, who exuded kindness like no one else could. Someone whom you couldn't help but love. Talking with Coz and Betty Ann at the wake yesterday afternoon, they spoke about Tessie's ability to get someone to come in to cover a shift. All the calls the night supervisor had made yielded no takers. No one wished to do it. Tessie struck gold on the first call and it had to do with this simple truth: "How could you say "no" to Tessie." There aren't many that loved and that respected that a no answer becomes an impossibility, but Tessie was that kind of person. Where did that love and that respect come from except from a person who epitomized caring, who exuded compassion like no one else could? Tessie was indeed someone whom you couldn't help but love.

If you ran your fingers across Tessie's name on her mausoleum crypt, there would come the memory of a nurse par excellence who left an indelible mark upon her patients, not to mention Sisters Hospital, the place where she applied her craft. If anyone was born to be a nurse, it was Tessie. It was in her blood. And I think it had a lot to do with the kindness and compassion that ran through her veins.

Her daughter Gail told me how nursing came to Tessie when she was sixteen, when she was given the responsibility of caring for her dying aunt. It served to inspire her to choose nursing as a vocation. It was interesting as to how her beloved husband John would always say that she looked better after a full week's work that she did after a full week's vacation. Nursing was never a job to Tessie. It was her life's calling. Even when she retired to spend more time with John, it wasn't long before she returned to work per diem, which, in a matter of months, morphed to full time labor.

And Tessie was so dedicated as a nurse that an eight-hour shift would never provide enough time for her to do justice to her patients. Time was never of the essence when it came to her bedside care. And it wouldn't be unlike Tessie to stop on her way home at the house of someone whom she knew had been ill. As much as she cared for patients, she cared as much for the people with whom she worked. They were her family as much as her patients were her family. She was often their guiding hand when problems arose. She was their role model, their go-to person when they had questions and concerns and difficulties. A proud graduate of Sisters Hospital School of Nursing, Tessie did the school and hospital proud in her care and treatment of the sick for what I believe was forty long years.

And also, if you rubbed your fingers across Tessie's name on the mausoleum wall at Hillcrest Cemetery, there would come to mind the memory of an unbelievable mother who was as good at motherhood as she was at nursing, who made it a point to plant in her children the same kindness and compassion that so marked her nursing life. Tessie, as many of you know, worked the night shift and so she'd often be coming home just when her children were getting out of bed. And she'd often share her day with them with the hope that in hearing of the sick, hearing of the emergencies, hearing of the dying, they'd come to realize what a blessing health happened to be and how fortunate they were to be free of the infirmities and pains that plagued so many people's lives.

Amy made mention of how, when reading books with her, she'd often cite a character with a problem and ask her feelings towards them, all in an effort to teach the importance of empathy. Tessie also made it a point to enroll Amy and Gail in programs and activities, doing so to expose them to as many things as possible with the hope of making them both a well-rounded person. She hoped that those programs and activities would help encourage them to be caring and compassionate as well as their becoming knowledgeable about what's enriching and important and valuable when it comes to life. And as good as Tessie was as a mom, she was even better as a grandmother. What Tessie tried to impart to her daughters, she did likewise with her grandchildren.

Tessie managed to convey to Laura her need to have feelings towards those less fortunate than herself, her need to always think how she would feel if she happened to be in their shoes.

Not unlike Laura's mom, those lessons left an indelible mark upon her soul and today Laura's students are the beneficiaries of the wisdom Tessie passed down to her favorite granddaughter.

If you were to rub your fingers across Tessie's name at the mausoleum at Hillcrest Cemetery, memories would come to mind of Tessie's travels home from the night shift or better said, her battles with sleep. One night John called the supervisor's office inquiring as to whether Tessie had left for home, and indeed she left hours earlier. John grew very concerned and was about to leave home in a frantic search of her whereabouts, only to discover her car in the driveway with Tessie in a sound sleep behind the wheel. Tessie became known to State Troopers and Police Officers between Sisters Hospital and Hamburg because it wasn't unusual for her to pull off the road and drive into a mall to rest her eyes, as she would say, a rest that often resulted in a Trooper or Officer banging on her car window to see if she was alright.

Then there was the famous day when she came to Mass at the Hospital Chapel and then thankfully before and not during my homily, fell sound asleep. When my homily came to an end, she awoke and began to applaud, believing she was in a theatre and a performance had just ended. Tessie's sleep stories would always generate laughter and if there was one thing Tessie enjoyed, it was her witnessing our smiles and our laughs.

So, my friends, Tessie Gornikiewicz is much more than a name on a mausoleum wall and if we are able to rub our fingers across her name, it would convey the memory of an extraordinary woman who exuded kindness and compassion; who was a nurse par excellence; who was a wonderful mother and grandmother and wife; who was a woman who exhibited the finest qualities you'd ever find in any human person. She left an indelible mark not only upon our souls and the souls of her many friends and patients and family, but also upon the soul of Sisters Hospital. Our lives, their lives, the institution of Sisters Hospital have been tremendously enriched because of it.

And the good thing, the great thing is that Tessie's life is not over. Our faith in the Lord Jesus Christ has let us know that when it comes to the end of a life, that life is changed and not ended, that when the body of our earthly dwelling comes to death, we gain an everlasting dwelling place in heaven. We are here today not just to celebrate Tessie's life but also to celebrate the fact that she's now enjoying eternal life and there will come a time when we will see her again.

DIAL 0

Tell of how it was that they exuded the tenderness, the love, the compassion, the warmth which that operator exhibited.

A prominent speaker in the United Kingdom once told of how, when he was six years old, his mother explained that if he ever needed help, he should dial zero for Operator and ask for information. One day, when the boy's mother was away, his pet canary, which always sang for him, seemed to be sick and unable to sing. He remembered what his mother had told him, so he dialed zero for Operator and asked for information and explained that his canary was ill. The Operator, who was wise beyond her years, gave him very helpful advice and it wasn't long before the canary began to sing once again.

Thereafter, every time he was alone and needed help, the boy would dial zero for Operator. Since he lived in a very small town, it was the same Operator who answered each time and the two became great friends. The day upon which his canary died the boy called the Operator in desperation, asking if there was anything he could do to bring his canary back to life and that kind and gentle woman comforted him and consoled him and said to him: "Remember this! There are other worlds in which to sing."

Years later, the young boy now a young man returned home from college. One of the first calls he made was to his old friend and upon dialing the phone he was disappointed when a voice he didn't recognize was on the receiving end of his call. The young man explained who he was, gave his name, and told how helpful and loving her predecessor had been especially when he needed help. The Operator, said to him: "I was told by Mrs. Jones, the former Operator that someday you might call. She told me about you when she was very sick. I'm sorry to tell you, young man, but Mrs. Jones has passed away, but she told me that if you ever called, I should tell you to remember there are other worlds in which to sing. And she wanted you to know that what was true for your canary was also true for her."

I tell that story because I could picture Kate being that operator. She had a warmth to her, she emanated tenderness, and she exuded kindness. As someone told me at the wake, she was a perfect combination of honey and sugar. If there was anyone in need of help, she was there. So, it would be just like her to reach out to that boy on the telephone to calm his fears and ease his anxieties, and to gently let him know that everything was going to be alright.

I'm not sure if it was Mike or Ann, but one of them told me that when Kate was four years old, she saw an elderly person with a problem, and it had to do with her teeth. Without batting an eyelash and with no squeamishness whatsoever, Kate ran up and helped her with those teeth, physically helping her secure them in her mouth, something most girls her age would find repulsive. When she was a mere kindergartner, she would put her change from lunch in the garbage can, figuring the homeless would find it as they did their nightly routine of going through trash cans. You could rightfully say that Kate had kindness in her DNA, she was born with a huge heart; within her from birth was this natural inclination to help other people. You could also say that if there was anyone born to work with the Special Needs Community, it was Kate Wirth. And for my two cents, I wish the church would wake up to the need to ordain women because Kate would've been the ideal priest. And she had the empathy to be a great one.

Besides the fact of her kindness loaded DNA, there was also the fact that no one could "light up a room" more so than Kate Wirth. She had a set of eyes that were not only beautiful, but which twinkled and which could melt away the fears and anxieties of anyone who came in contact with them. She also had a million dollar smile, a great sense of humor and an ever-positive spirit.

Her laughter was contagious. To have her in your company was, without question, a wonderful blessing.

And no one had a good time as well as Kate. She loved to dance and sing and entertain. She was the life of every party and someone who made it a point to make sure everyone was having fun.

Yes, indeed, we lost one heck of a beautiful person a few short days ago and many, many people are grieving her absence, many, many hearts are heavy with grief. Consolation, I believe can be gained by referencing the message that operator left for that young man in my opening story. Although Kate Wirth's song is no longer being heard, she is still singing but is doing so now in another world.

And that world was described with the words: "Eye has not seen nor ear heard nor has it entered the hearts of people to know what the Lord has prepared for those who have loved him." Our faith tells us that that world is our destiny. Our faith tells us that when we die, life is changed not ended and when the body of our earthly dwelling lies in death, we gain an everlasting dwelling place in heaven. Kate is now in God's celestial kingdom where peace and happiness eternally dwells. She's enjoying the company of her sister, Kara Mae and her grandparents Bill and Marge Wirth. And the good news is that there will come a time when we will see her again.

THE WINDOW

Tell of how, in bearing the heavy cross of their particular illness or debilitation, their focus was on us and not themselves, how they somehow managed to remain positive and endearing.

A most moving story was penned by G.W. Target, entitled *The Window*. Its setting was a hospital room which had two beds at opposite ends of each other and one window. The window was placed in such a way that only one patient in one of the beds could look and see out the window. Two patients in that particular room were very sick. The man who was able to see out the window regularly reported to the other man what he saw. He talked about the weather, the cloud formations, and the pedestrian and vehicular traffic. Some of the people he saw, he saw with such regularity that they began to discuss the person.

For example, there was this red-haired girl who walked by at 10 a.m. every morning. One morning, she was hurrying and between the two of them they decided that she had a new job and she mustn't be late.

Then there was a nun that came by at about 10:30 every morning, always with another nun. One morning she came by with a gentleman. They were engaged in earnest conversation. The two patients talked about that one for quite some time and decided that he was her brother visiting from out of town.

The man who could see out the window reported on how the paper boy was gaining better accuracy tossing his papers. And he also told about the little children and the games they played and the pranks they pulled. Then, of course, there was the nurse who met this gentleman every day at 4:30 p.m. in the front of the hospital. Then, all of a sudden, she wasn't meeting him anymore. They couldn't decide about that one, whether the two had broken up, or maybe got married and no longer pursued the niceties of romance.

In any case, the man who could see out the window reported it all to the other man. In a sense, he labored hard to bring the outside world into view for his roommate who had become his friend. Then, one day, his condition worsened and soon thereafter he passed away.

It was but a few hours later that the patient in the other bed, deeply grieving the loss of this one with whom he had been sharing so much for quite some time, thought that perhaps he'd gain some comfort by moving to the other bed, that maybe by looking out the window and seeing those things and activities which his friend had regularly reported seeing, that maybe it would help ease the pain of his loss which weighed heavy upon his soul. So, he asked to be moved.

The nurses moved him, tucked him in, and made him quite comfortable. The minute they left, he propped himself up on one elbow painfully and laboriously, and he looked out the window. And there, but twelve feet away stood a dark gray wall.

I beg your indulgence for telling that lengthy story, but it's one that has always moved me and I'm sure it moved more than a few of you. And that's because it's the story of someone in the midst of their own pain and suffering, laboring hard to ease the suffering and pain of another. It's the story of someone who is hurting, pushing aside his or her pain to make life more livable and bearable for a friend.

It's a story reflective of Linda Bujalski. Throughout her two-year fight with a rare and insidious cancer, throughout her many trips to the hospital and the doctor's office, she not only pushed aside her own hurts and pain to make life more livable and more bearable for her friends and family, but she also pushed aside her own hurts and pain to make life funnier, to make life more beautiful, to make life more humorous for her family and friends.

Take the time when chemotherapy shed her hair. There were days that she'd come to work with her wig on sideways just for laughs and she even wore a blue wig just to get a charge out of one her workmates. When the doctor took tumor biopsies and sent them to California, she quipped as to how at least a part of her would make it to the West Coast. She even liked that joke about the patient who got bad news from his doctor. The doctor told him that he has Alzheimer's disease as well as cancer. The man replied: "Thank God I don't have cancer."

I think it was her dad that tabbed her as a verbal Zorro, which meant she could trade zingers with the best of them always with the flare of humor. One of the funnier things she did was submit Jim's name for that show: *Queer Eye for the Straight Guy*. That was because Jim hadn't bought a new suit or shirt or tie in over five years.

Linda's Mom told me that as a child Linda was always bubbly and that continued on throughout her adulthood, throughout her entire life and it continued even through her illness. And so besides humor being a regular part of Linda's repertoire, so was her zest for life, so was her excitement for all that life had to offer. I'm not sure who told me this but apparently when Jim and

Linda first saw the ocean, before Jim had a chance to take off his sunglasses, Linda was already running up and down the beach.

Then there were her shopping trips, one of the passions of her life. She'd shop in a whirlwind manner, shopping more for the benefit of her sister and family than for herself. Linda would often sneak in naps so that when Mike would come home from day care, she could care for him and love him with the same vigor and zest that marked the days when she wasn't sick.

And besides her humor and her vitality, you also had her extraordinary talent. She was a great artist. She could draw wonderful sketches freehand as well as with the computer. She was a talented piano player, often serenading little Mike with her music. She even gave thought to authoring a book, hoping that before she died she could publish a book to help kids deal with the problems that come when their mom has cancer.

And probably Linda's greatest and most wonderful of qualities was her unselfishness, her care for others, her concern for everyone but herself. When she learned of her dire diagnosis of cancer, she kept the full story from her parents not wanting them to worry. She was so glad to be able to take Michael to Disneyworld for she so wanted him to enjoy the fun of that magical place. She packed a lot of living into the short time that was her life and so much of it was aimed in the direction of helping and aiding the people she loved.

She truly was like that man in the hospital bed facing that window. Despite her dire condition, she did all she could to make life happy and good and normal and wonderful for her family and friends. I believe that one can truthfully say that Linda Bujalski was one beautiful and extraordinary human being.

In the Muir Woods of California, a phenomenon takes place every once in a while, involving one of those giant Redwood trees. When one of those trees are logged, blown over, or destroyed by fire; in other words, when one of those giant trees dies, the seeds which the tree produced for years, the seeds which are spread all over the ground below the tree, those seeds miraculously begin to sprout all around the place where the tree once stood. Forest Rangers say that there are three reasons why that occurs. The trauma of the tree's death stimulates growth hormones within the seed. Second, they are now able to absorb the sunlight which was previously blocked by the tree. And third, they get moisture and nutrients from the tree's root system which still remains intact even though the tree is gone.

I believe that you can say that James and Michael; David and Mary Anne Borgioli; David Jr. and Mary Ann; Ed and Pat Bujalski; and many of you here; you are the seeds Linda has left behind. Just as Linda has now entered into new life in the resurrection of our Lord, so are you brought into new life, a life without her wonderful presence. But thanks to what Linda was to all of you, thanks to the treasured memories of a beautiful and heroic life, you have sunlight, and you have moisture and nutrients to help your new life along. Linda Bujalski is gone but she'll always remain rooted in the lives of those who had the privilege of having her life touch theirs.

THIS IS YOUR LIFE

Tell of whose voices might have been heard and the stories that might have been told, had the deceased been the chosen celebrity.

Those of you sporting a bit more gray than I may well recall the television show *This is Your Life*. It aired from 1952 to 1961. Its host and producer was a fellow by the name of Ralph Edwards who upon a stage would greet an unsuspecting celebrity who had no idea as to what was about to transpire. Edwards would introduce him or her to the audience and then suddenly he'd shout the celebrity's name and with the same velocity he'd bellow: "This is Your Life."

A voice would then be heard from backstage. Its owner would tell a story or describe an incident from the celebrity's past. That voice might've belonged to his or her mom or perhaps their third-grade school teacher or a next-door neighbor or an old friend. The owner of that voice would then appear on stage and be reunited with the celebrity guest. The scene would keep repeating itself

34

till the entire stage was filled with a vast assortment of his or her friends and acquaintances who, from what they had said from backstage, created for the audience a collage, a scrapbook, a series of snapshots that told not only of what had steered that celebrity into the direction their life had taken but revealed as well the type and sort of individual the celebrity guest happened to be.

Caught by surprise on that Ralph Edwards show were such stars as Stan Laurel, William Frawley, Johnny Cash, Max Sennett and many others who happened to have held celebrity status back in that era.

Now, had Ken been a celebrity and had he graced the stage of that Ralph Edwards Show: *This is Your Life*; many voices would've been heard from beyond the black curtain and at the end of the show, the stage would've been filled with all sorts of individuals who provided the audience with a picture of whom Ken happened to be.

The audience would've heard of how Ken was a member of what Tom Brokaw called "The Greatest Generation." He was in the Pacific theater of operation during WWII and participated in the famous Battle of Midway. Like so many did back then, he left behind security and family to fight for our country.

That audience would've heard of how church was a big part of Ken's life. He served as a trustee of this parish and, as far as church ranking is concerned, a layperson cannot hold a more prestigious church position. Ken was also a faithful and giving member of the St. Vincent DePaul Society and he was a tireless worker when the Catholic Charities campaign got underway. A few short years ago, he was presented with the St. Joseph the Worker award for all the work he had done on behalf of this parish. As someone said: "If Ken doesn't go straight to heaven, then there's no hope for any of us."

Had Ken appeared on that show *This is Your Life*, the audience would've heard of what a great father he happened to be. I understand that there was a plaque that adorned a wall in Ken's home which read: "Anyone can be a father, but it takes someone special to be a dad." Ken was most certainly someone special. You couldn't come upon a more loving father than he, a more giving

35

father than he. And prominent on his fatherhood resume was the heroic act of taking his children and their screaming friends to a Beatles movie back in the 1960's.

That audience of *This is Your Life* would've also heard of what a terrific grandfather and great-grandfather he happened to be. He would make his grandchildren laugh every chance he got, even if it meant putting his false teeth in and out when the grown-ups in the room weren't watching. And Ken wouldn't be averse to scaring them, of striking fear in their hearts with his running tale of an alligator lying in his backyard just beyond the drainage grid. And when it came to candy, grandpa had a bottomless stash, as the candy dishes in his home were never empty. But most importantly and most especially of all, Ken gave his grandkids and great grandkids the example of how a life should be led: His generosity, his humility, his forgiving spirit, his ability to bend with the times, never complaining about how things weren't as they once had been, his kindnesses towards everyone, his great range of interest and actions, his ability to cook and bake, his positive outlook on life. Ken could well be called a Renaissance Man and as such, Ken's grandkids and great grandkids could not find a greater role model when it came to the way they should live their life.

Had Ken appeared on that show: *This is Your Life,* the audience would've heard as to how he'd often be found humming big-band tunes and church hymns and how he famously painted many a picture, many of which now adorn the walls of his children's homes.

The audience would've heard of how he loved "Manhattans" and scratch off lottery tickets and breakfast at the Holiday Showcase. How he was the most affable and the most eligible bachelor, one of the most loved residents of the Elderwood Nursing Home where he spent the last years of his life. The audience would've heard of how he kept up his contacts and friendships with the people from the old neighborhood where he started his life, and how his management of life over the thirty some years since his wife's death spoke volumes as to his resourcefulness and courage.

And then just when the curtain was about to drop onto the stage of *This is Your Life*, the audience would've heard voices tell of what a wonderful man Ken happened to be and how you'd be hard-pressed to find someone who could match Ken when it came to integrity and honor and moral fortitude.

Yes, indeed, if back in the day, had Ken been a celebrity and had appeared on the television show *This is Your Life*, the audience at the end would've been so enamored by the things they heard that they'd have wished that they had known him, for had they known him, they would've been richly blessed.

We're gathered here today not just to honor and celebrate Ken's life, but to celebrate the fact that his life is not over. Jesus let us know that when we die, life is changed not ended and when the body of our earthly dwelling lies in death, we gain an everlasting dwelling place in heaven. Ken is back together again with his wife Loretta and his parents and his brothers and his girlfriend Bobby. And I wouldn't doubt that God's got him working in the halls of heaven, perhaps making gourmet German dinners for all of German persuasion who had preceded him in death.

THE FORK

Tell of their culinary skills and varied ways their life was blessed beyond measure.

I recently came upon a wonderful story about a man known far and wide for his generous and grateful spirit. Though diagnosed with cancer and given but a few months to live, he still maintained the twinkle in his eye and his terrific sense of humor, and still regaled his friends and his family with his wit and with his wisdom.

Well, this man went to see his pastor to talk over his funeral arrangements. He said: "Listen Father, I want to make sure that everything is going to be upbeat when I'm brought to church for my funeral mass. After all, I've had a pretty upbeat life, I've been truly blessed, and I've been enriched beyond measure by my family and my friends. So, there is nothing to be sad about. So,

Father, be sure to play lively hymns and be sure to select hopeful Scripture passages and as far as my eulogy is concerned, I'm going to help you."

"How are you going to help me?" The pastor asked. "Well, let me tell you," said the dying man. "I'm going to help you in that I plan to be laid out at the funeral home with a fork in my hand. As you know, Father, I love to eat, and you are aware of all the suppers I've attended. What you don't know, however, is that my favorite part of any dinner is when they begin to clear away the dishes and someone leans over and says: 'You can keep your fork.' That tells me that a piece of pie or cake is about to come, and I love cake and pie more than I love steak or lobster or pork or chicken.

So for me, when they say 'keep your fork,' it tells me that something better than what I've just ate is about to come. So, Father, when it comes time for my eulogy, you can make mention of that fork I had in my hand while lying in the casket and which I'm sure that everyone noticed and talked about. You can tell the folks what I've just told you. You can tell them on my behalf that I'm very grateful for the rich and wonderful life that I've led, but I'm keeping my fork because I know that something even better is about to come."

I began with that story because, first of all, it speaks of our faith, a faith which tells us, as that man noted, which tells us that when we die, new life awaits us, and that new life is far better and far greater than the life that had come to an end.

The second reason I began with that story is because a fork was a big part of Mary's life. Mary was a great cook. Amongst her favorite dishes were potato salad, cheese potatoes and Beef Wellington. As good as she was as a cook, she was also a great baker. Her Christmas cookies were to die for, not to mention the cakes and pies which she magnificently prepared.

And besides her prowess as a cook and as a baker, Mary also enjoyed the other side of the table, especially the dessert side. She loved her cookies, her sponge candy, her dark chocolate, and anything and everything that was sweet and yummy. It's been said that she qualified as a bona fide chocoholic.

The third reason I began with a story that I did was that, like the man in the story, Mary lived a blessed life. First of all, she lived into her late 80s. She lived her full lifespan and got ten bonus years besides and, with the exception of all her medical issues over the past six months, she enjoyed a relatively healthy life.

Mary also was blessed with a great family. She raised five boys, Bill, Jim, Kevin, Dan and Jeff, and raising those five boys qualified her for a Purple Heart. But as trying as raising those boys had to be, she did it well and they've done well.

And thanks to where some of her boys chose to settle, she got to travel. She made it to Anchorage, Alaska for her granddaughter's wedding and she got to escape the Buffalo cold by visiting Dan and his family in Florida. And she even got to Sicily and was able to see where her parents and grandparents had lived.

And nothing made her happier than the days when her boys blessed her with grandchildren, nine in all, and then felt doubly blessed when those nine grandchildren provided her with 16 great-grandchildren. Mary was blessed with a great family which she enjoyed and who in turn enjoyed her. And the highlight of every year was the family reunion she hosted, not to mention numerous backyard get-togethers and Mary's not to miss New Year's Eve party.

Mary was also blessed with many good friends, two of whom took her to Hawaii and then surprised her with a party for her birthday. And she liked nothing more than going to the Senior Center where she met her friends on a regular basis and took part in friendly games of pinochle. You had to ask yourself as to whether she went to the Center because of her friends or did so because of the pinochle.

And being the giving person that she was, Mary got involved in the local food pantry as well as the Italian Club as well as the American Legion Post Auxiliary. Mary was not one to sit still, so she loved volunteering in every way she could and thanks to the volunteering, she made even more friends. And because of her being a kind and loving and giving self, because of all the good she did for so many, I believe it could well be said that the world today is a little bit darker because Mary is no longer here to give it light.

So, when all is said and done, Mary lived a blessed and wonderful life and it was enriched beyond measure by her family and her friends. And the greatest thing of all is that her life is not over, her dessert has arrived. She's now enjoying a greater life with no more pain and suffering, a life where her mind is clear, and her vigor and vitality have been restored. And that life will never come to an end. She's now in God's celestial kingdom where peace and happiness eternally reigns, reunited with her beloved husband and her parents and so many others who preceded her in death. The good news for us is that there will come a time when we will see her again.

LAUGHTER

Tell of their humorous nature, describe their positive qualities.

A man from Chicago left its cold and snowy weather for a sunny vacation in Florida. His wife, who was on a business trip, was expected to join him the next day. After settling in a Florida hotel, the husband decided to send his spouse an e-mail. As it turned out, he had misplaced her e-mail address. Trusting his memory, he typed in what he believed was her address and with it a message. But unfortunately, he was one character shy of the exact address, and the message went out instead to an elderly widow of a preacher who had died the day before. When the grief-stricken woman checked her e-mail, she screamed, then fainted. Her family members rushed into the room and discovered these words on the computer monitor: "Dearest wife, just got checked in. Everything is prepared for your arrival tomorrow. P. S. Sure is hot."

A recent study reported that laughter entices the brain to produce a drug called dopamine, a morphine like painkiller, and in observing patients recovering from orthopedic surgery, it was indeed found that the more they laughed, the less was there need for pain medication.

It's been shown that laughing a hundred times a day is the cardiovascular equivalent of 10 minutes of rowing.

Dr. Patch Adams, whom Robin Williams made famous in a movie by that name, does his hospital rounds dressed in a clown costume and other outrageous attire with the intention of provoking laughter amidst his patients because, as he saw it, laughter did therapeutic wonders.

Lee Martin did therapeutic wonders. Lee Martin relieved a lot of pain. Lee Martin provided us with the exercise equivalent of 10 minutes of rowing. And he did it with his corny jokes, he did it with his great smile, he did with his humor, he did it by infusing the lives of those around him with a great deal of laughter.

Nothing pleased Lee more than to see people laugh. Nothing brought him more joy than to see a smile on the face of those around him.

Lee was a hard man not to like. His easy-going manner, his willingness to do anything for anybody, his multiple likable qualities, his refusal to say 'No' when help was needed; that made him a hit wherever he went, that made him somebody you were always glad to see. That made him someone of which it could be said that a party was not a party unless Lee Martin was there.

That, coupled with his love of family, his love for his children, his love for his grandkids, his love for all the women in his life; that made him one remarkable and beautiful individual whose absence is going to put a big hole in many a person's life.

Now, the one thing that irks all of us, the one thing that bothers us all is that Lee left life too soon. Lee got robbed of the full bank of years usually allotted to a life. That being so, it's going to be up to us to fill in the years Lee didn't have. It's going to be up to us to carry on for him all the wonderful qualities of living that he had shown to us.

There's a story I've told a thousand times. It concerns a painter by the name of Sir Edwin Landseer. He painted murals and one of his greatest works of art adorns a wall in a tavern in Scotland. On the day when the mural was being dedicated, a bottle of champagne accidently popped, sending a stream of bubbly liquid onto the mural. Dead center, a dark stain appeared. Efforts to clean it were of no avail and all determined that it had been ruined.

When the last guest left the party, Sir Edwin went downstairs and retrieved all the paint he had used in the mural's creation. He made that dark stain into a rock and then had a waterfall splash its waters upon it and he made other changes to the mural so much so that the mural was more magnificent than the original. The stain which could've ruined a beautiful painting ended up adding to the painting's beauty.

Those wonderful qualities of living that Lee had shown to us is what I would call the paint Lee left behind for us to use for that stain on our hearts, the stain that got placed there when Lee passed away a few days ago. Now, if we can use that paint to make something of the stain on our hearts, if we can use that paint to make our lives more beautiful, in other words, if we can bring smiles to people's faces and get them to laugh, if we can love as Lee had loved, if we can make it a point to say yes to people's needs, if we do all of that, then we're making sure that Lee's life doesn't end here because people will see Lee living on through us.

A great writer and churchman, C.S. Lewis, once wrote something that he claimed he could've never written before because he'd have considered it sentimental claptrap. He wrote that since his dear friend Charles Williams died, heaven was no longer a strange and far off place. It had been that once, but now it was a dear and familiar place because his friend was there.

Our faith tells us that when we die, life is changed, not ended and that when the body of our earthly dwelling lies in death, we gain an everlasting dwelling place in heaven. Lee lives on now in God's celestial kingdom where peace and happiness eternally reign.

Can you imagine the golf courses Lee is now playing? Can you imagine the hockey rinks where Lee is now skating? And then how about the endless supply of Tim Horton's coffee and "twisted tea" he's now enjoying?

Lee Martin is now in heaven and so I believe, like CS Lewis, I believe we can say that heaven is no longer a strange and far off place for any of us because our friend Lee Martin is there.

The country-western group Lonestar has a popular song of which I believe many of us are familiar. It's called *I'm Already There*. It's a song about a man in a lonely cold hotel room who misses his family. He calls home and tears well up in his eyes as he hears the sound of his kids laughing in the background. One of the kids gets on the phone and says: "Daddy, when are you coming home?"

It's then that we hear that song's beautiful refrain. It goes: "I'm already there, take a look around. I'm the sunshine in your hair. I'm the shadow on the ground. I'm the whisper in the wind. I'm the moonlight shining down. I'm the beat in your heart."[4]

That man in that lonely cold hotel room is telling his family that although he may be a thousand miles away, he's still there. All they need to do is take a look around.

Lee Martin is not a thousand miles away, he's a whole world away. He is now in that place of which the Holy Spirit said: "Eye has not seen, nor ear heard nor has it entered the hearts of people to know what the Lord has prepared for those who loved him."

Though Lee is that far away, he's still here with us and all we need to do is take a look around. Be it the whisper in the wind, be it the shadow on the ground, be it the moonlight coming down, be it any of the places that Lee would frequent, he is there, and he will always be there and one day we will see him again and enjoy his love.

GOING TO HEAVEN OR HELL?

Tell of the positive things that could well have been heard by those who attended the funeral.

There is a story out of India regarding a Zen master who, being tired from a long walk, took shelter on a porch outside a home that

4 Lonestar, "I'm Already There," June 2001, track 7 on I'm Already There, BNA Records Label, compact disc.

happened to be located a short distance from a cemetery. Inside the home lived an old lady and her grandson. While the Zen master rested, he couldn't help but notice a funeral procession heading down the street toward the cemetery. He then heard the old lady shout to her grandson: "Go down to the street and find out who that is and where they're going." The boy ran and joined the funeral procession and, after it made its way to the cemetery, he came back and announced to his grandmother: "It's an elderly gentleman and he's going to heaven."

The Zen master wondered how the boy came to that conclusion but, before he could knock on the door to ask, another funeral procession was going by and once more the grandmother told her grandson to go and find out who it is and where they're going. The boy did as he did before but this time when he returned, he said: "Grandma, it's a middle aged woman and she is going to hell."

Well, the Zen master couldn't believe the boys ability to tell a soul's destination and so he called for him and asked him: "Son, how are you able to determine as to whether the dead person is going to heaven or hell." "It's simple!" said the boy, I go and join the funeral procession and listen to what the people who are following the body are talking about. In the first case, they were saying: 'What a wonderful man he was, how he was helpful and gracious and kind, how they lost a good friend, how you couldn't find a better man than he." "Everybody was saying such nice things about him," said the boy, "I figured where else was he going but to heaven?"

"What about the second case?" asked the Zen master. "Well," said the boy, "when I walked in that procession, all I heard were people grumbling about how terrible a woman she was, how she never had a kind word for anybody. I even heard a few say: 'I'm glad she's gone!' I figured, after hearing that, where else was she going but to hell?"

I don't think there's any question as to where John Farr is going. If that young boy had walked in his funeral procession, he'd have heard many good things. He'd have heard many wonderful things. He'd have heard how John took the long road

44

to get his bachelor's degree and did so with academic distinction; how his pursuit and accomplishment of that goal served as an inspiration to many.

He'd have heard many in the twelve-step community praising his perseverance and cherishing his friendship and ever grateful for the support and encouragement he gave to so many. If that young boy had walked in John Farr's funeral procession, he'd have heard about how John took good care of his mother, Mary Ann, and how he was a tremendous source of help and comfort to her in her battle with the various ailments that plagued her life.

He'd have heard how well thought of he was at the Erie County Department of Social Services, how he was not only a valued employee but a friend and confidante to many. His work was so stellar that he achieved many a promotion and the Department looked forward to his completing his master's degree, for they saw bigger and better things in John's future.

If that young boy had walked in John Farr's funeral procession, he'd have heard how he brightened many a person's day with his humor, his knock-knock jokes, his ability to bring smiles to people's faces and provoke laughter within their hearts. He'd have heard as to what a sweet, thoughtful, kind and intelligent man he was, how good he was to his nieces and nephews, how he took the time to say hello and share bits of humor to those having a bad day, how he served the church as a Eucharistic minister, how he could be counted upon for warmth and support and good cheer, how he was one of those rare individuals who could make you smile and laugh just by being around him.

Yes, indeed, if the boy in my opening story had walked in John Farr's funeral procession, he'd have reported back to his grandmother that John was going to heaven, because he'd have told her that everyone in that funeral procession had nothing but good things to say about him, nothing but wonderful things to say about him.

My friends, we're gathered here today to mourn John's death but also to celebrate the fact that he has begun new life. He's begun the resurrected life promised by Christ Jesus. John made it into the halls of heaven, that place of which the Holy Spirit said:

"Eye has not seen, nor ear heard, nor has it entered the hearts of people to know what the Lord has prepared for those who have loved him."

John's probably gotten a big bear hug from his good friend Father Stanton and he's met up with his grandparents and his brother Richard. I would think that he and Father Stanton have a lot of catching up to do, and perhaps from their perch in heaven, the two can pull the strings necessary to get the Sabres and the Bills back into the playoffs.

I've been told that there's been a debate going on in theological circles ever since the beginning of time. The debate is over the issue as to whether there is laughter in heaven. One school of thought says there is no laughter in heaven because the whole point of heaven is serene contemplation of the truth and the beauty of God. The other school of thought is that there must be laughter in heaven because God wouldn't have it any other way. As I see it, theologians can debate that question all they want. I know for a fact that there is laughter in heaven. I know it because John is there and if John is there, you can bet there will be laughter in heaven.

MEMORIES

Provide a review of the good memories the deceased had generated.

A good number of you are old enough to remember how you had to wait at least two minutes for the television to warm-up, how you got your windshield cleaned and oil checked, and your gas pumped without having to leave your car, how when you bought a box of laundry detergent, it wouldn't be unusual to find a free glass or a dish or a towel inside the box.

A good number of you are old enough to remember when a quarter was a decent allowance, when a 57 Chevy was everyone's dream car, where store products came without safety caps and hermetic seals, when being sent to the principal's office was nothing compared to the fate that awaited you when you returned home.

Many of you are old enough to remember when you never had to lock the front door, when war was a card game, when eenie, meeny, miny, moe was the key to decision making, when race issues had to do with how fast we ran.

A number of you are old enough to remember Nancy Drew, the Hardy Boys, Howdy Doodie, the Peanut Gallery, the Lone Ranger and Tonto, Roy and Dale Evans and their horse Trigger.

A good number can remember candy cigarettes and wax Coke shaped bottles with colored sugar water inside, Blackjack and Clove chewing gum and Pine Brothers cough drops, the "candy" we were allowed to eat in school.

A good number of you are old enough to remember home milk deliveries, newsreels before movies, telephone numbers that began with words, party lines, hula hoops, 45 RPM records, green stamps, treasure chest coupons, Lincoln Logs, 15 cent hamburgers, Studebakers, washtub ringers, Tinker Toys, the Fuller Brush Man, five cent packs of baseball cards with that awful layer of bubblegum inside, erector sets, pop guns and roller skate keys.

Those of you old enough to remember many of the things and places and people I've just mentioned will well agree that though they are for the most part distant memories, they can be recalled at any moment and at any time and when they're recalled, it's as though they're still a part of life today.

Memories are one of the gifts God has given us to show how what happens to be gone isn't really gone at all; how what's passed out of existence still manages to make an appearance upon the stage of life. Death may have robbed us of the person we loved, but it can't steal our memories and as long as we have memories, so our loved one will continue to live on, or so will it seem as though they had never left that stage of life.

When it comes to Joseph Hirtzel, we have many memories, memories which will warm our hearts and soothe our souls and bring smiles upon our faces. Mary will forever remember the day a Maryknoll missionary in Japan connected her with Joe when he was on an R&R trip during the Vietnam War. It must have been love at first sight, because they've been together ever since. Mary will remember how, many years ago, when she was working as a tour guide in Niagara Falls, Joe got to meet the other Japanese tour guides and Joe, being the generous and considerate individual he happened to be, realized that Thanksgiving was near and their families were back in Japan and so, unbeknownst to Mary, he invited them all to his house for Thanksgiving dinner. That began a Hirtzel family tradition of opening the family table and taking in any travelers or visitors on Thanksgiving Day.

Midori and Mayumi will always remember their dad as wearing a smile and being so gregarious that he would engage strangers in conversation, whether it be in the checkout line of the grocery store or just passing by on a street corner. As I understand it, Joe worked the counter for Eastern Airlines. I guess you could say Joe was born for that job. By nature, a people person, he knew how to talk to people, and his penchant for listening and taking time with each individual, made him a public relations jewel. He would assume that job at the front desk of St. Joseph Hospital. Eastern Airlines and St. Joseph Hospital were lucky to have someone like him dealing with the public, which we all know at times can be a very difficult and arduous task.

Midori and Mayumi will always remember the conversations they had with their dad on a multitude of issues especially during the commercial breaks of a Star Trek rerun. They'll forever recall his love of reading and learning and his great range of knowledge, knowing of subjects as obtuse as aviation technology, as deep as ancient cultures and rituals, and as mundane as the Buffalo Bills and Buffalo Sabres.

Joe's sisters Alma and Sue will never forget their years growing up with Joe and how supportive he always was for whatever they set out to do. Joe will forever be remembered as a man of great faith. He was an altar boy at Most Holy Redeemer Parish and he was a regular at my Sunday mass at St. Joe's hospital.

Joe will forever be remembered as someone who took pride in his work, who had a great spirit, who loved this country, a proud serviceman during the Vietnam War. And Joe will be forever remembered for his valiant fight against cancer, for his unbelievable endurance of various chemotherapies and various setbacks, taking it all in stride and never allowing it to deflate his positive spirit.

Joe will especially be remembered as a loving husband, a great father, a wonderful brother, a devoted son, a caring friend, an Eastern airline devotee, and especially, a wonderful man.

God has given us all the gift of memories not only to bring smiles to our faces and warmth to our souls, but also to help us to realize that what's gone still manages to live on, that when someone we love dies, that life continues. And it continues not only in our memories, but it continues in a resurrected existence where peace and happiness eternally reigns.

Joseph Hirtzel lives on now in God's celestial kingdom and we're consoled in the fact that he's not hurting anymore, that he's not in any more pain. He's reunited with his parents and so many of his friends and family who preceded him in death. Joe will not be physically present anymore, but he lives on and one day we will see him again.

A MARVELOUS LIFE

List the qualities of their life one can marvel about.

I recently read as to how many years ago our ancestors would go out walking, usually on a Sunday afternoon, sometimes alone, sometimes with a spouse, sometimes with the whole family. And they called it going marveling. They would look for unusual rocks, unusual wildflowers, seashells or even four-leaf clovers, whatever could be labeled as marvelous things. They would collect them, bring them home and then show off the marvelous things to all whom they were close to and near.

I don't know of anyone or any family that goes out marveling. I don't know of anyone or any family who will go out on a Sunday in search of marvelous things. And it's a shame, because there's much to marvel about.

Take a walk through the local art gallery, a walk-through a State Park, a ride over a country road on a late fall afternoon, or paddling a canoe in the waters of the Adirondacks. In each and every one of those marveling possibilities, you may not have been able to take things back with you to show off to your family and your friends, but in each and every one of those marveling possibilities you could go back to your family and friends and tell them that you had viewed some unbelievably marvelous things.

And if that isn't in the realm of possibility, if that kind of marveling is beyond your reach, you can try rubbing shoulders with special people. You can get in touch with and get to know people who are extraordinary, people who are a step above the rest, people who can get you to stand up and applaud the minute they enter a room.

Do that and you'll have a lot to marvel about. Do that and you can go back to your family and friends and tell them that you had viewed and got to learn about a life that exhibited many marvelous qualities.

Take Lt. Thomas James Eugene Crotty, whom we've come to remember and honor here today. If you had rubbed shoulders with him, if you would have gotten in touch with and gotten to know him, just think of what you could marvel about.

You could marvel at his athletic ability; he was one of South Buffalo's greatest athletes. He coached and managed and played on an American Legion Junior baseball team which captured the 1929 National Championship. He was a whiz at basketball, outstanding in football, and he would serve as the captain of the Coast Guard Academy football team. In whatever sport he chose to play, Jimmy was a standout. He exhibited extraordinary athletic ability.

Also, if you rubbed shoulders with and gotten in touch with and gotten to know Jimmy Crotty, you could marvel at his leadership abilities. While attending the Coast Guard Academy, he was elected class president in his freshman year, class vice president and also company commander in his senior year. In 1940, he was appointed Special Deputy Marshal representing the Justice Department on the Bering Sea Patrol. Jimmy also took charge of a clandestine effort to strip and detonate the USS Sea Lion, a damaged American submarine, thus keeping it out of the hands of the Japanese. He was second-in-command on the Quail, a minesweeper, and from its deck coordinated the bombardment of Japanese forces on the Bataan Peninsula. Lt. Jimmy Crotty commanded many a high-risk mission. He took charge of many an effort to thwart Japanese activity. In whatever job he tackled, Jimmy played a leading role.

If you had rubbed shoulders with and gotten in touch with and gotten to know Jimmy Crotty, you could marvel at his intellectual prowess. Not only did he excel in his studies at the Coast Guard Academy, but he undertook a course of study at the Mine Warfare School in Virginia and later at the Navy's Mine Recovery Unit in Washington D.C. Thanks to his intellectual prowess and his ability to absorb all that he was taught, Lt. Jimmy Crotty went on to become the Coast Guard's and the US Military's leading expert on explosives.

And then there is Jimmy's devotion to duty, another thing to marvel about. That devotion to duty is what would propel him to legendary status. One of his high-risk duties involved his commanding two small motorboats that went into the bay in the dark of night, drawing a chain between them so to sweep out hidden mines that could well have sunk any Allied vessel that came through those waters. Another one of his high-risk duties had him, on numerous occasions, risking his life as he ferociously defended Corregidor Island from Japanese invaders. Jimmy's devotion to duty was off the charts.

If you had rubbed shoulders with and gotten in touch with and gotten to know Jimmy Crotty, you would've marveled at how beloved he happened to be. You would've marveled at his embodiment of the Coast Guard values of honor and respect and dedication. You would've marveled at all the medals he was awarded, all the accommodations he received. You would've marveled as to how a South Buffalo boy went on to achieve hero status, how a South Buffalo boy could be seen by the entire country as one of the greatest soldiers that ever lived.

Now admittedly, it is a shame that, unlike our ancestors, none of us go out on a Sunday afternoon looking for marvelous things, that unlike our ancestors none of us go marveling anymore.

But it we ever decide to do so, if we ever decide to go marveling, we don't have to go to the Botanical Gardens or Letchworth State Park or take a canoe ride down the Allegheny River, or a ride across the Rainbow Bridge. All we have to do is go out and get to know and rub shoulders with someone of the likes or of the caliber of a Jimmy Crotty, someone who led a life where there's so very much to marvel about.

We are gathered here today not just to remember and honor Lt. Thomas James Eugene Crotty, but we here as well to celebrate his coming home to South Buffalo, his coming home to this parish where he went to school and where he worshiped.

We are here as well to celebrate his faith, a faith that tells us that though Jimmy Crotty died of diphtheria in a POW camp on the Philippine Islands on July 19 of 1942, his life was changed, it didn't come to an end, because on that July day he entered the resurrected life that Jesus promised, a life that all of us will someday enjoy when we join him in God's Heavenly Kingdom.

A WONDERFUL LIFE

Review the places, the organizations, the committees, the individuals who would be bereft and impoverished had he or she not graced the stage of life.

This very day draws to a close the Christmas season and so I'm given the liberty of referencing a yuletide illustration, in particular, the Frank Capra's movie classic: *It's a Wonderful Life*. We all know the story. George Bailey, played by James Stewart, lives in the fictional town of Bedford Falls N.Y. where he marries a beautiful girl, starts a family, and finds success as the owner of a Buildings and Loan Association. Hard times strike the banking industry and when George's Uncle Billy loses a bank deposit of $8,000, it appears the Building and Loan Association would have to close and with it would come bankruptcy, scandal and prison time for George Bailey. Totally distraught, Bailey considers taking his own life, figuring the insurance money would cover that $8,000 loss.

As he stands on a bridge intending to jump, his guardian angel Clarence Oddbody appears, hoping to convince him not to do it. George complains to Oddbody that the world would be better off without him, that the world would be better off if he had never been born. Clarence decides to show him that it wasn't true. As George heads back to town, he gets to see how bereft Bedford Falls would be and how impoverished many a life would be had he, in fact, never been born. The movie ends with George Bailey in the parlor of his house surrounded by his family and all his many friends. They had anted up the money to save the bank and it was in testimony to all the wonderful things he did on their behalf. George Bailey comes to realize that the world wouldn't have been better off without him. He'd come to realize that he had in fact lived a wonderful life.

William George Stanton lived a wonderful life and the fact is that many a place would be bereft, many a life would be impoverished, had he never been born. Take St. Bridget's Parish in Newfane, New York. Its parishioners would never have realized the fruits of empowerment, they would never have come to the understanding that they and not the pastor were the church, that the responsibility for the running of the parish rested in their hands.

One of Bill's favorite stories involved a meeting of the personnel board. He and the other members of the board were interviewing several candidates interested in the pastorate of a particular parish. The process concludes with a vote taken by the board as to whom would be the best man for the job. The results are sent up to the bishop who makes the ultimate appointment. Well, in the course of an interview of a particular priest, Bill asked him what his thoughts were as to a parish council, what his thoughts were about empowering people. The priest barked back: "You mean like Newfane!" Bill, who was pastor at St. Ambrose at the time, said: "Yes, I guess you'd say like in Newfane." "You left the place a mess!" said the priest, "The people there think that they own the place!" The priest in question called Bill the following day to apologize. Bill accepted the apology but then informed him that "he voted yesterday". The parish and the people of St.

Bridget's Church in Newfane would be greatly impoverished had Bill Stanton not been born.

If Bill Stanton had never been born, many a life of an alumnus of Bishop Turner High School would have been greatly impoverished. As many of you know, Bill spent many years at Turner as a teacher as well as the vice principal and that latter role carried with it the responsibility of administering discipline. I can think of one kid in particular who probably possesses the best attendance record at his present place of employment thanks to Bill's creative disciplinary tactics. The kid I'm referring to had the habit of missing school on Mondays and one Monday, Bill had a little extra time on his hands. He goes to the kid's house and knocks on the door. His grandmother answers and she's glad to see him because her grandson had gone back to bed once his mother left for work, and he wouldn't respond to her pleas for him to go to school. Bill asked her where his bedroom happened to be and went right to it. Upon entering the room, Bill pulled the kid out of bed and threw him onto the floor. (A more memorable wake up call I'm sure he'd never had.) Bill says to him: "Get dressed, you're going to school!" When he got the kid to school, he parked his car in the farthest extremity of the parking lot so he could parade him past several classroom windows, driving home the point to anyone who saw them that they'd better perish the thought of ever skipping school.

Along with such "over the top" disciplinary tactics were the ones Bill gleaned from the Marquis de Sade. Students deft at spitballs might be found on all fours pushing a spitball down a long corridor with their nose and misbehaving in general often resulted in the guilty party kneeling in a squat position reading poetry for a half an hour at a time.

One of Bill's favorite tactics was to have the wayward child come to his office. While the kid would be waiting to see him, Bill would be loudly barking orders to his secretary (with tongue-in-cheek, of course) asking that she put together transfer papers for Kensington High School. She was also to look up the boy's father's work number so the father might be informed of the transfer. The kid, hearing all of this, would be beside himself in fear and terror. When he'd finally get called into Bill's office, he was like putty in

Bill's hands. He'd be begging for mercy, promising never to give misbehaving a second thought.

There are many a Bishop Turner High School alumnus in the community who have Bill to thank for keeping them on the straight and the narrow, who have Bill to thank for giving them guidance and direction and inspiration, who have greatly benefited from the wisdom and the example and the care which Bill provided them. Many a life of a Turner High alumnus would be greatly impoverished had Bill Stanton never been born.

And so, it can be said for many a life of a Sister of Mercy. I've lost track of who is presently on the Mercy leadership team but I'm willing to bet that each one of them was taught at one time or another by Bill Stanton. In Bill's early years as a priest, he was a regular instructor of the novices of the Mercy order. His teaching style, his charisma endeared him to many and especially so was the fact that he was their window to the outside world. Back in the days of old, novices couldn't read newspapers, listen to the radio or watch television. So, whenever the novice mistress left the room, Bill would stray from his lecture and begin commentating on the news stories of the day. He'd relay to the novices the goings on of the Vatican Council, the results of local elections, and the teams participating in the World Series, as well as tantalizing bits and pieces of neighborhood gossip.

And besides being their teacher, Bill was a confidante and a confessor to many a Mercy novice and left an indelible mark on many of their hearts. What most won him their admiration and appreciation was his advocacy of the role of women in the church. Bill trumpeted many a feminist cause and didn't let a Vatican ban stop him from talking about women's ordination. Many a life of a Sister of Mercy would be greatly impoverished had Bill Stanton never been born.

And so would the Diocese of Buffalo be greatly impoverished as well. I don't know how many of you are familiar with Bill's younger days as a priest, but back then he helped found and then lead a group known as the Priest's Association. The Association was comprised of priests not at all pleased with the way some of their brothers had been treated by the chancery office nor were they at all pleased about some of the positions the Diocese had taken on some of the more important issues of the day. The Association made a lot of noise and rattled more than a few cages and their doing so gave much strength and comfort to many a disgruntled priest as well as many a disgruntled Catholic. As you might well imagine, the Association was not a favorite of Bishop James McNulty as the two fought many a battle. Bill got labeled as "a crafty politician" by Bishop McNulty and, interestingly enough, also labeled as "one of his finest" by the very same Bishop shortly before he would die.

In the friendlier days of Bishop Head, Bill served several terms on the Priest's Council and was elected as its president for a good portion of his term. Thanks to his leadership, many a welcomed change was made to better this Diocese. Yes, the Diocese of Buffalo would be greatly impoverished had Bill Stanton not been born.

So, too, would be the presbyterate of this Diocese. I don't need to tell you that Bill was a great mimic. He could mouth the stereotypical accent of each and every nationality and wasn't averse to using that talent to fool and trap unsuspecting priests. I can remember his calling a mutual friend of ours who had just been named pastor of an Irish parish, with his patented Irish brogue, pretend to be a parishioner decrying the German heritage of the new pastor. The guy fell for it hook, line, and sinker.

There were also the famous Priest's parties where a few glasses of Dewar's and soda would prime Bill to do his famous Bishop Leo Smith imitation, Smith being the Diocesan Chancellor at the time. It wouldn't be long thereafter when his buddies would get him to call one of the priests and as "Bishop Leo Smith" inform him of a change of assignment usually to a parish where the priest would have dreaded to go. Some went so far as to pack their bags only to be informed at the eleventh hour that the great mimic Stanton had scored again.

And besides his being a great mimic, Bill was also a masterful storyteller and would regale us for hours with stories which, though we had heard ten times over, never lost their humor. He'd love to tell of the antics of Monsignor Leo Toomey, the legendary pastor of St. Teresa's Parish. A favorite was the time someone swore at Msgr. Toomey while he was directing traffic in front of the church. He caught the license number of the car and later asked Bill's dad, who was a police officer at the time, to trace it to its owner. Bill's dad did not have the heart to tell him that the car belonged to the pastor of the neighboring parish.

And besides the entertainment he provided for many a priest of the Diocese, he also modeled for them excellence in ministry. A priest extraordinaire for the entire length of his priesthood, he stood out from his peers in many different ways. Many a priest came to him for counsel, many saw him as a mentor, and many sought his wisdom when tangled in the web of a difficult pastoral problem. The priests of the diocese would be greatly impoverished had Bill Stanton never been born.

And this parish, our parish, would be greatly impoverished had Bill Stanton never been born. Who will ever forget Bicentennial Sunday, July 4th of 1976, when Bill celebrated his first mass here at St. Ambrose? I was on the altar with him and, though we were friends, I had never heard him preach. After he read the Gospel, I remember sitting down to listen to his sermon only to find him exiting the pulpit and heading out into the congregation. Here was this 52-year-old man running up and down the aisle as though he were on fire. He filled the church with an electricity most of us had never seen or experienced before. He spoke with such enthusiasm and conviction that even the most comatose of parishioners raised their heads in attention. A model of church and worship got set into motion that weekend and our lives have been dramatically altered for the better ever since.

Think of the way he empowered us to take charge of this parish. Think of the courage he had to raise issues and advocate for causes that weren't very popular here in South Buffalo, how he often spoke a truth few of us wished to hear. Think of how he was always there when we needed him, at our house if someone we loved died, at our bedside if we were sick, and in a chair nearby when we needed to cry. Think of the tremendous eulogies he gave for so many who had died and how so many of us hoped he'd live long enough to preach at our funerals when the day of our death arrived.

Think about how he made us laugh, how he pumped so much joy into our parish. He must have told us a thousand times how his family used to live on Roanoke Parkway but then they got a little money and moved to a place off Abbott Road. That always brought laughter no matter how often it was said. Or how about his telling us how people call me "Duke" because I came from Polish nobility. Or how about the true story of how, when John Paul II was elected Pope, I was too absorbed in making out my baseball line up to care. Speaking of Popes, my one regret is that Pope John Paul II didn't die before Bill. Bill was a student of the papacy and, whenever Papal elections were held, he was in his glory. Papers would be strewn across his desk with biographies of the Cardinals, and he'd carefully handicap their chance for election with an opinion or two as to the politics of the process. I'd imagine that when the day of Pope John Paul II's death finally arrives, Bill, from his perch in heaven, will do what he can to influence the choice of his successor.

Think of how Bill both inspired us and at the same time broke our hearts as for the past two years he pushed himself to do ministry despite pain and discomfort, despite looking haggard and tired and worn, how he pushed himself to continue his commitment to say Mass and deliver outstanding homilies each and every Sunday. My God, how impoverished we here at St. Ambrose would be if Bill Stanton were never born.

And how impoverished Peg Stanton would be and Sheila and Eileen and Ellen and Maureen and Patti and John. Bill loved his family. They were his pride and joy. He loved to visit Peg on his day off even though he'd sleep in her Barcalounger for hours on end.

And finally, if Bill Stanton were never born, my life would be greatly impoverished as would be Jack Wiemar's and Pat Keleher's and Jim Croglio's and Jack Connif's. Bill was more than a friend; he was a mentor, a sage, role model, a sounding board, and a giant in the priesthood. He was a Renaissance man. He helped make us who we are and brought out the best that was within us. Our lives would be terribly bereft had Bill Stanton never been born.

So, when all is said and done and when you put it all together, Bill Stanton had a lot in common with the mythical George Bailey. Had he not been born; many a place would be bereft; many a life would be impoverished. Bill indeed had lived a wonderful life and not just a wonderful life, but also a saintly life, an extraordinary life, a magnificent life, an unbelievable life.

You might recall that at the end of the film *It's a Wonderful Life*, George Bailey's brother Harry toasted him as the "richest man in town". I toast all of you today. You are the richest people in the world because you were a part of this man's life.

SAINTS

Tell of the many ways they brightened someone's day, tell of how they were the 'sunshine' of many a life.

There was a little boy who came to church with his mom. While she was lighting candles and attempting to pray the stations of the cross, he was doing what little kids do in church, he was running around examining just about everything. After a while, she called for him and he didn't answer. She looked around and saw that he was in the sanctuary looking at the stained-glass windows.

The sun was streaming through, and he was fascinated as he moved his hands back-and-forth with all the different colors rolling across his face and onto his clothes. The mother said: "Come, we have to go! But he didn't budge." So she walked up to where he stood.

There was a statue to his right and he said to his mom: "Who is that?" and she said: "That's Jesus." The boy pointed to another statue and said: "Who's that?" And his mom said: "That's Jesus' mother." And he then pointed to the stained-glass windows and said: "Who are they?" And she said, "They are the saints." The two of them then headed home.

The next day in school, the teacher made some references to saints and the little boy got all excited. The teacher didn't know what to make of his reaction and so she asked him why he was so excited. The little boy blurted out: "Teacher, I know what saints are! I know what saints are! They are the ones that let the sunshine through them."

Now I do not believe that the Holy See would ever give consideration to naming my Aunt Helen Osuch a saint. But if we follow the criteria for sainthood as described by that little boy, she most definitely qualifies. Through the course of her lifetime, my Aunt Helen did let a lot of sunshine through her. She brightened many a life.

Think, if you will, as to how she lit up every room she walked into. My Aunt Helen was the essence of elegance. She always looked like a million dollars, her hair always perfect, her clothing exquisite, just enough makeup to heighten the beauty of her face, and a demeanor that commanded respect. She comported herself in a way that made everyone feel at ease, that made everyone feel like family, and she exuded a positive energy that lifted everyone's spirits.

And not only did my Aunt Helen light up every room she entered, but she also injected sunshine into many a life. Her first husband Matthew, we called him Uncle Sandy, was one of the nicest guys you'd ever meet. I can remember him arranging for the Knights of Columbus to be honor guards at my ordination. And I believe his positive spirit, his being a nice guy, had a lot to do with my Aunt Helen and I'd bet that if he were alive today, he'd tell you that she was the sunshine of his life.

And as fate would have it, or as God would have it, my Aunt Helen ran into Eddie Osuch whom she had not seen in years. There was an almost instant revival of the love they once had for each other that dated back to their high school years. I had the honor of conducting their marriage and more than a few would say that my Aunt Helen turned up a light in him that had grown dim since the passing of his first wife. My Aunt Helen lit up his life just like she did the life of my Uncle Sandy. And if he were alive today, I'm sure he would say that my Aunt Helen was the sunshine of his life.

We're going to hear from her daughter Sandra later in this Mass, and I'm sure she'll testify as to how her mom lit up her life. If you talk to Devon her granddaughter, she'd tell you much the same. She will vouch for the good vibrations that emanated from her grandmother's life. You could say that my Aunt Helen injected sunshine into the lives of her entire family. And the sun not only shone through my aunt into the lives of her family, it did as well into the lives of many a stranger and many an acquaintance and many a neighbor and many a friend.

I believe you all know my Aunt Helen's sewing history. She learned the trade while nursing her daughter and she saw knitting as the answer to her desire for fine clothing. And wanting to spread the wealth of her knowledge to others, she opened a sewing school and that attracted thousands who not only learned the trade of sewing, but became the beneficiary of my aunt's positive spirit. A natural for television, she became a regular on AM Buffalo where her winning smile and gorgeous looks lit up the screens of televisions all across Western New York. And like those who attended her sewing school, those who viewed her on television also became the beneficiaries of her positive spirit. Through the vehicle of sewing, my aunt became the sunshine of many a life.

And not only was my aunt Helen the essence of elegance who radiated positive energy and lit up every room she walked into and every life she encountered, she also had a big and a generous heart. No one logged as many volunteer hours as my Aunt Helen did. Whether it be at the nursing home where she lived, the Kiwanis Club, the Polish National Alliance, the Polish Arts Club, my aunt made it a point to give back to the community. She never forgot her Black Rock roots or her Polish heritage and how blessed she was to grow up in a family that gave so much to her. Because she had been blessed, she felt obligated to go out and bless others.

In so many different ways, whether it be her charm, her demeanor, her positive spirit, her good vibrations, her generosity, her care, my Aunt Helen lit up many a life. My Aunt Helen brightened up many a life. My Aunt Helen was the sunshine of many a life.

So, I believe it goes without saying that my Aunt Helen was a saint, not a saint as far as the Vatican is concerned, but a saint as far as that young boy in that classroom is concerned, she let a lot of sunlight shine through her.

And the greatest thing of all is that my aunt is now in a place where the sun always shines. We learned as a Christian people that when we die, life is changed not ended and when the body of our earthly dwelling lies in death, we gain an everlasting dwelling place in heaven. My Aunt Helen is now enjoying new life in God's eternal home and there will come a time when we will see her again.

UP

If he or she possessed a scrapbook, what would be the snapshots that would most definitely be included? Describe the wonderful adventures, the dream trips upon which they embarked.

A movie years ago won an Oscar for animated films. It was of such high quality that it got nominated for an Oscar for the best picture of the year. I'm talking about *Up*, a film from the animation wizards at Pixar Studio.

It begins with one of the most touching and poetic four minutes ever seen on the silver screen and all told without a word of dialogue. A quiet kid named Karl meets Ellie, a real spitfire. They both dream of going on a great adventure to a faraway place. The two of them grow up, fall in love, marry, and transform a ramshackle house into their dream home, all the while putting their loose change in a big glass jug, hoping to eventually use it to finance the adventure they longed to have, the dream trip they were hoping to take.

As luck would have it, home and car repairs and medical bills kept emptying that big glass jug. Nonetheless, Karl and Ellie are happy and, in an instant, they are celebrating their 50th wedding anniversary. Shortly thereafter, Ellie would succumb to cancer leaving the grieving Karl lost and alone.

After Ellie is gone, Karl finds the scrapbook Ellie kept since she was a little girl. It was called *My Adventure Book*. The first pages are filled with the silly, funny little treasures and memories of childhood. Then there's the page Ellie labeled "Stuff I'm Going to Do" and it was on the following pages that Ellie planned to chronicle the adventure, that dream trip she and Karl were hoping to take, and Karl is stung with remorse that he never kept his promise to take Ellie on that trip.

As Karl turns the page, he sees that Ellie had collected pictures of their life together, their courtship and wedding, their working side-by-side on their house, the simple joys of going out for ice cream together. On the final page under one of the pictures of the two of them together, Ellie wrote in bold letters: "Karl, thanks for the great adventure, thanks for the dream trip, go out and have a new one, love, Ellie."

It was at that point that Karl realized that although they never went on their great adventure to a faraway place, although they never went on the dream trip financed by the loose change from that big glass jar, they had their dream trip, they had their great adventure. It was their many happy and wonderful years which they spent together.

Now if Marty Breen ever kept a scrapbook, it would be something along the line of that one that Ellie put together. It would be filled with photographs of a life well lived. It would be filled with many a picture of the wonderful adventure, the dream trip that was Marty's life.

There would be a snapshot of a map of Ireland. Not only were trips to Ireland one of the joys of Martin's life, but so was Irish literature and so was Irish history. Marty saw great value and unbelievable richness in his Irish heritage. And he never let a moment pass where he didn't promote Irish culture in any way that he could.

In Marty's scrapbook, you would, of course, find a picture of Mass Mutual Life Insurance Company. Fifty years with one company is almost unheard of today, but that was the length of time that Marty spent with Mass Mutual. And he distinguished himself as one of that company's most valued and honored employees as he held numerous jobs at virtually every level of the company. For thirty-three years, he was the recipient of the National Quality Award. He was a yearly member of the

Million Dollar Club. He was probably the most conscientious, the most honest and one of the most respected individuals in the insurance business. And I daresay that Mass Mutual wouldn't be the company it is today if not for the mark he left on almost every facet of the insurance operation.

In Marty's scrapbook, there would be a picture of Canisius College and South Park High School. Marty, as many of you know, was passionate about almost everything he touched along life's way. He did not just attend both of those schools but, in the years that followed, he did what he could for the schools' benefit. A distinguished football star at South Park High School, he got involved with the alumni, trumpeting whatever the cause that would better the school. And at Canisius College, Marty was instrumental in getting faculty and administration and alumni and student alike to work together to promote understanding, to cherish differences, to respect opposite views, and to develop a social conscience. Marty saw the Alumni not as a group of back slappers, but an integral piece of the education process. He was so well thought of and so well respected and so revered by Canisius College, there is little wonder why he was named Canisius College Man of the Year or why he was named Distinguished Member of the D Gamma Society or why he was tabbed for the school's Board of Directors as well as the Board of Regents. Canisius knew they had someone special when it came to Marty Breen. I daresay that Marty's due diligence on behalf of the school is one of the reasons for its positive reputation, one of the reasons as to why Canisius has held fast to its morals and its principles.

If Marty had a scrapbook, there would be the pictures of his five children: Marty Junior, Lauren, Brian, Kevin and Allison. There would be the pictures of his seven grandchildren, his two stepdaughters Jeanne and Deborah, not to mention his brother John and his sisters Patricia and Eileen as well as numerous nieces and nephews. Family was big in Marty's life, and he enjoyed their company, and he enjoyed most especially the numerous reunions. He enjoyed being a part of the life of every member of his family. As far as Marty was concerned, his life was enriched beyond measure thanks to his family.

If Marty had a scrapbook, he would have a picture of two prominent women: Jean O'Neill and Lupe Lepino. Marty was blessed with two wives, each of which complemented him beautifully. Lupe wrote of how when they first met, they had so much in common that they couldn't stop talking. He was the first generation of Irish parents, and she was the first generation of Spanish parents. Both were successful in life and both shared mutual interests. The relationship had all the earmarks of a marriage made in heaven and so it proved to be. After a whirlwind courtship, they sealed their bond, I believe, at the altar of this very parish. And what a wonderful time they had together engaging in conversations and mutual volunteering and sharing love and sharing heartache.

If Marty Breen had a scrapbook, there would be a picture of a pen. Marty was a distinguished author. He penned numerous bylines for the insurance industry, and he had a byline in the Buffalo News dedicated to life insurance underwriters. He wrote two books, one entitled: *Lizzie and Other Stories from an Irish American Boyhood* and the other entitled: *The Fighter and the Dancer* which takes you through a history of Irish life here in Buffalo going back to a previous generation.

Next to that pen in that scrapbook would be Breen's Tavern, located right outside the corner of this church. Marty grew up in that Tavern. It was the backdrop of the stories Marty told in the book *The Fighter in the Dancer*.

And I daresay that if Marty had a scrapbook, there would've been a picture of Sisters Hospital where he served as a lector for my morning Masses and a Minister of the Eucharist in our Skilled Nursing Facility. And then finally, in that scrapbook, there would be a picture of Kyoto, Japan where Marty served as a member of the Military Police just after the Second World War.

If Marty Breen had a scrapbook, you would've seen all the photos as providing a testimony to Martin as a loving father, a devoted husband, an extraordinary grandparent, a distinguished author, an insurance magnate, an award-winning Alumni of South Park High and Canisius College, a Renaissance man, a renowned storyteller, a man of impeccable honesty and integrity and conscientiousness, a man of great taste and good humor and a wonderful temperament, a man who left his mark in so many different places and in so many different ways, a man of whom it was an honor to claim as a friend.

And if you were to look to the last page of Marty's scrapbook, you would've seen in bold letters: "Thanks for being a part of the wonderful adventure, the dream trip that was my life." And then beneath that would be the words: "Go out and start a new adventure and take a dream trip without me."

Although Marty Breen's earthly adventure is over, his heavenly adventure has just begun. Jesus died and rose from the dead to assure us all that when we come to death, life is changed not ended. Marty is experiencing now the kind of life of which the Holy Spirit said: Eye has not seen, nor ear heard nor has it been in the hearts of people to know what the Lord has prepared for those who have loved him. Marty is reunited with all those who preceded him in death and with whom he is now enjoying eternal life.

BACKDROP TO OUR SPOTLIGHTS

Provide examples of their "behind the scenes" role, how they happened to provide the backdrop for the spotlights which many a life had occupied.

Frank Boreham is an Australian preacher who wrote in the early part of the previous century. I found his books to be literary jewels. They are collections of sermons he preached while in the active ministry that spanned many decades. In one of those books, there's a sermon where Boreham talks about famous writers and artists and the people responsible for their fame.

Reflecting on William Wordsworth, he mentioned how when Wordsworth was in danger of entangling himself in the military and political troubles of the time, it was his sister Dorothy who recalled him to his desk and pointed him along the road that led to his destiny. It was she who reawakened in him a craving for poetic expression.

Referring to Robert Louis Stevenson, Boreham wrote of how a certain Fanny Sitwell taught him to believe in himself, how when he struggled with poverty and even death itself, it was she who convinced him to carry on. It was she who supported him, cared for him and kept him focused on his work.

And then there was Vincent van Gogh, who had a brother named Theo who helped him find his talent and did what he could to nurture it along.

History records no special place for Dorothy Wordsworth or Fanny Sitwell or Theo van Gogh. There is not a poem or a piece of prose or a painting that bears their name. Yet without their behind-the-scenes presence, without their behind the curtain work, we would never have heard of William Wordsworth or Robert Louis Stevenson or Vincent van Gogh.

Now, I am not sure if any of Helen Moran's children or grandchildren will ever occupy a spotlight in history, but if they ever do, it will be because of Helen Moran. Helen was a Dorothy Wordsworth, a Fanny Stillwell, a Theo van Gogh kind of person. She never occupied the spotlight. She wasn't someone who commanded much attention. She never achieved a great deal in terms of personal wealth or prestige. She was a background type of person, a behind the scenes kind of individual. She, in a very quiet and unassuming way, nurtured the good and helped unravel the gifts and talents of each and every member of her family.

Be it the lunch that was always ready when any of the boys, whenever Kathy came home from school. Be it her ability to sweet talk their father out of whatever punishment he thought necessary for whatever deed they may have done. Be it the faith in God she transmitted or the good that shined forth from her life. Be it the way she stretched the milk money and the food money to accommodate the extras: the candy, the class trips, school supplies, and the movies they so wanted to see. Be it the parties for grandkids which she delighted to host or their birthday parties or their Christmas parties. Be it the walks to the milk machine at Ridgewood and South Park Ave. Be it her attendance at Morgan's Irish dances on St. Patrick's Day. Be it her presence at the major events of all of her family's lives. Be it the prayers she said, the little things she did, her willingness to do anything for you, her gentle and kind demeanor, her attention to details, the warmth she generated, the kindness for which she was responsible, Helen Moran, from her background position, from her behind the scenes location was indeed a major player in the lives of each and every member of her family.

She was the Dorothy Wordsworth, the Fanny Stillwell, the Theo van Gogh to Jim, Terry, Kevin, Brian, Tom and Kathleen as well as her 10 grandchildren and two great-grandchildren. She was the backdrop to their spotlights, the person who very quietly and unassumingly played a role in their achieving what they've achieved, in their becoming what they've become, and in their garnering the blessings they happen to enjoy.

I don't believe there is anyone here who has not seen or admired the inspiring picture of the praying hands. It was Albrecht Dürer's most famous work. There's a remarkable story behind the painting. It turns out that Albrecht and another young artist found themselves in financial difficulty and couldn't afford to stay in school. It was determined that one of them would get some menial job to support the other. When one became a success, then the other would be able to study.

Since Albrecht seemed the more talented of the two, his friend spent the next year at all sorts of hard labor. In the meantime, Albrecht completed his studies and began to sell his art and was finally in a position to help his roommate. By that time however, the hands of that self-sacrificing young man were so gnarled and scarred from the hard jobs he took on, he could no longer hold an artist's brush.

One fateful day, Albrecht came home to find his friend in prayer, and he started to sketch those well-known hands, the hands that made it possible for him to pursue his career.

Those praying hands could well be the hands of Helen Moran. She worked hard for many years. She sacrificed a great deal so all of her family might realize their dreams. Whenever you see those praying hands, think of Helen Moran and thank God not only for her, but for the many like her who are part of the backdrop of the spotlight we may happen to enjoy.

We are gathered here today not only to pay tribute to Helen's wonderful life but also to celebrate her new life. We believe as a Christian people that when we die, life is changed not ended and that when the body of our earthly dwelling lies in death, we gain an everlasting dwelling place in heaven. We just celebrated Easter which calls to mind the rising of Christ from the dead, a rising God promised to all of his people. Helen is now present in the halls of heaven, enjoying a blessed reunion with her daughter Kathleen and her husband Jim and so many friends and family who preceded her in death. She's not physically present anymore, but she lives on and one day we will see her again.

THE DOCTOR AND HIS DOG

Tell of what they'd wish for us to do, how we can carry on from where their life had ended.

In one of his books, John Braille tells of an old country Doctor who made his rounds in a horse-drawn carriage. The Doctor's dog would go along for the ride. One day, the Doctor went to visit a man who was critically ill. "How am I, Doctor?" the man asked. The Doctor replied: "It doesn't look good!" Both men were quiet for a while. The man then said: "What's it like to die, Doctor?" As the old Doctor sat there trying to think of some words of comfort, he heard his dog coming up the stairs. And then, because the door was shut, the dog began to whimper and scratch at the door. The Doctor said to the man: "You hear that? That's my dog! He's never been in this house before, he doesn't know what's on this side of the door, but he knows that his master is in here. And because of that, he knows that everything is alright. Now," said the Doctor, "death is like that. We've never been there, and we don't know what's on the other side of the door of life. But we know that our master Jesus Christ is there and, because of that, we know that everything will be alright."

I begin with that story, first of all, because it spoke of a dog and Pat loved dogs and he would've appreciated the canine reference. And second, Pat's faith was such that when death took him a few short days ago, he wasn't afraid. He knew Jesus Christ would soon be meeting him on the other side of the door of life and, because of that, he knew that everything will be alright.

Although everything is alright with Pat, everything is not alright with us because we lost someone we had loved very much. Even though it can be said that he's not suffering anymore and he's not hurting anymore, the fact that he was only 68, the fact that he got robbed of the full lifespan, doesn't sit well with us. So, we are upset and grief filled and now we have to learn to live without him.

Now if there's one thing that Pat would ask of us, if there is one thing that Pat would be concerned about, is that we don't mope about his death, that we make the best and most of our life despite the fact that he's no longer here.

One of my stories which I've told many times is that of a painter by the name of Sir Edwin Landseer. His greatest claim to fame is a mural that happens to occupy a wall of a famous Tavern in Scotland. On the night when that mural was being dedicated, a bottle of champagne exploded and splashed upon the mural, causing the paint to run. Efforts to clean things up failed, and there, right in the middle of this beautiful mural, was this big dark black stain.

Everyone thought the mural was ruined, but when the last guest left the party, Sir Edwin Landseer went downstairs and retrieved all the paint he used to paint the mural. That black stain, he made into a rock, and then from that rock he painted a waterfall and he made other changes in the mural so much so that the end result was a mural that was more beautiful and more magnificent than the original. So that stain that could've ruined a beautiful painting in the end added to the painting's beauty.

Pat's death has left this black stain upon all of our hearts, especially upon Sheila's heart, his wife whom he loved so much. Especially upon the hearts of his children Christine and Susan and Patrick. Pat's death also left a stain on the hearts of his sister Maureen and his brother Kevin, his two nieces, his nephew, his cousins and all the friends he made throughout the course of his life.

The challenge for all of them, for all of us, is that we make something of the stain. And when you look back on Pat's life, he's left behind a lot of paint. He's left behind plenty of examples of positive living that can well be used to make something of the stain.

Think if you will, of the great care which Pat provided his family. Think if you will of how he gave of himself for the sake of others, the way he gave of himself to this parish. The pews you are sitting in, the windows in the classrooms above us all bear Patrick's mark. Think as well of how he gave of himself for the kids he taught, going so far as to run for the school board to help better their education. (We won't mention how he exploited his kids to make that happen with Christine and Susan holding up signs that read: "Vote for my daddy.") Think if you will of how Pat happened to be the kind of guy that would give you the shirt off his back. Think if you will of Pat's dedication to the students, he taught at Hutch Tech. Think if you will of the excellence demonstrated in applying his skills as a wood crafter and how proud he was of the things he built.

So when you look back on Pat's life, when you look back at his unselfishness, his dedication to duty, his giving ways, his striving for excellence, his love and his care for others, his good humor, his love of parties, his love for fun; they can all be seen as the paint Pat's left behind for all of us to use to make something of the stain his death placed upon our hearts.

And if we do that, if we reflect back in our life the wonderful and positive qualities that were evident in Pat's life, it's about the best tribute we could ever pay to him, the most fitting memorial you could ever erect in his honor.

We are gathered here today, not only to recognize and call to mind Pat's wonderful life, but also to celebrate the fact that he's begun a new life, a life free of pain and a life without the struggles to breathe and walk. Jesus died and rose from the dead to let us all know that when we die, life is changed not ended. And when the body of our earthly dwelling lies in death, we gain an everlasting dwelling place in heaven.

Pat is now in the company of all of his family and friends who preceded him in death. He's seeing places more beautiful than Lake George; he's visiting museums now that will knock his socks off; and he's seeing galaxies far greater than those in any Star Trek film or episode. And we're all hoping that now that he's in heaven, he can do something to help the Buffalo Bills end their playoff drought.

There's a popular song by the country-western group Lonestar. It's entitled *I'm Already There*. The song centers on someone in a lonely cold motel room who misses his family. He calls home and when he hears his kids laughing in the background, tears come to his eyes. Then a little voice comes on the phone asking as to when he was coming home. It's then that we hear the song's beautiful refrain:

"I'm already there, take a look around, I'm the sunshine in your hair, I'm the shadow on the ground, I'm the beat in your heart, I'm the moonlight coming down, I'm the whisper in the wind."

That man in that lonely cold hotel room lets it be known to those he loves that although he's miles away, he's still there with them. All they need to do is to take a look around.

Pat is not miles away; he's a whole world away. He's in that place of which the Holy Spirit said: "Eye has not seen, nor ear heard nor has it entered the hearts of people to know what the Lord has prepared for those who loved him."

Though that may be so, Pat is still with us and all we need to do is take a look around. Be it the moonlight coming down, the whisper in the wind, the beat in our hearts; be it the halls of Hutch Tech, be it this very church, be it any of the places where Pat left his mark, he's there and will always be there and there will be a time when we will see him again face to face in God's eternal home.

THE LUCK OF ROARING CAMP

Tell of the places that felt their loss, the positive effect they rendered upon the lives and communities that happened to be blessed by their presence.

Although Zane Grey ranks as America's greatest Western novelist, author Bret Hart is not far behind. Amongst his many works is a short story entitled *The Luck of Roaring Camp*. The story involves a group of miners whom you might best describe as morally and hygienically challenged. They cussed a lot. They showered infrequently. They never shaved. They settled their disputes with fists. They drank excessively. They were known to get raucous and nasty. And since women were not allowed in their camp, courtesy and cleanliness were not high on their priority list.

One day a woman named Cherokee Sal came into the camp seeking medical help. She was nine months pregnant. Before any of the men could react or help, she birthed her child and then died shortly thereafter. So, to this raucous, dirty, unkempt group of men fell the challenge and duty of caring for the baby.

They placed the child on some clean rags, and then placed her in a shoebox and immediately realized the box wouldn't do for a baby as beautiful as she. So, a miner was sent fifty miles on a mule to purchase a Rosewood cradle, the best that money could buy. Upon his return, they scooped up the child and gently placed her in the cradle only then to realize that those clean rags were not the kind of bedding material befitting such a beautiful child.

So, the same miner who purchased the cradle was sent back those fifty miles to buy the daintiest and the softest lace he could find. When the baby was laid in her new cradle with this most beautiful and daintiest of lace, the men noticed with dismay something that escaped their attention and that was the filth that covered the floor. So, they scrubbed the floor only to then realize that the walls needed painting and the windows needed to be fixed and cleaned and that beautiful curtains were now a necessity. With all that accomplished, the miners then realized that behavioral changes were in order.

The baby needing rest, the men couldn't be as raucous as they once had been and, with the beautiful baby in such close proximity, their use of four-letter words had to stop. They needed to make sure their scruffy faces and bearded chins didn't scare the child, so they began shaving and showering and cleaning their clothes and began looking more like men going to Sunday School than men working a coal mine.

In a place called Roaring Camp, a baby comes upon the scene and the entire camp undergoes a wonderful and positive transformation.

Much like that infant in that mythical story, whenever Jim came upon the scene, in whatever camp he would set foot inside, a positive transformation would indeed take place.

Consider his place of employment for many long years, Import Motors. Ask those with whom he worked about the impact he had upon them, and they would tell you that they're a better man or a better woman thanks to his being there. His smile, his pleasant demeanor, his optimism, his love for people was contagious. It rippled through all the facets of the business operation. Those under his charge and all those to whom he reported began to gain the sense that they were all a family. Thanks to Jim's presence, Import Motors was transformed from a place of business to a place that felt like home.

And those who came there to service their car, they felt that sense of family, that sense of camaraderie. And if they had the good fortune of interacting with Jim, they would be the better for it. And when it came to their car, they'd never go to any place but to Import Motors because they knew Jim would be there not only to take care of their car, but to take care of them as well. Although Jim worked for just a brief time with Volkswagen Motors, that camp was the better for it too. He was making the same impact there as he had made at Import Motors.

And could you ever think of a man more suited for an Usher's job than Jim? Whether it was taking tickets, serving as a teller at the racetrack, or showing people to their seats; if he knew you, a hug was in order and if he didn't know you, he acted as though he did. Like that baby in Roaring Camp, people who came in contact with Jim even for a brief instant were the better because they did. He'd brighten their day with a smile. He'd emit positive energy and infuse joy into their souls just in the way he handled your ticket or ushered you to your seat.

And if anybody needed something, if something happened

to be broken, if a mechanical problem was in evidence, Jim would be the first one there to help and he came cheap; a Labatt's Blue and a bag of chips were all that he'd accept as payment. And besides getting your problem solved, besides getting what was broken fixed, you were the beneficiary of his smile and his warmth and his humility and his optimism. Your day was made not just because he took care of the problem, but because he was there. And he always made it look like you were doing him a favor instead of the other way around.

And besides making their day and brightening the lives of those with whom he worked and whom he touched through work, he did the very same thing when it came to his family, when it came to Kim, Megan and Tim.

Kim will never forget meeting Jim at a house party. It was love at first sight. Her life was brightened beyond measure for over 29 years, thanks to Jim. Megan and Tim remember their dad as a great communicator and how, for their dad, Thanksgiving was the biggest day of the year, not because of turkey and football, but because he felt so blessed and was so thankful for his kids and his wife and his family.

So, when all is said and done, when you look at the big picture of Jim's life, it does in many ways parallel the life of that baby in Roaring Camp. Just as that baby transformed Roaring Camp immeasurably, just as that baby positively impacted the lives of those miners; so did Jim transform immeasurably and positively impact the places where he worked and the places where he lived and the lives of all whom he touched throughout the course of his life. When you come right down to it, hundreds of lives would be terribly bereft, they'd be greatly impoverished had Jim not set foot inside their camp.

We are gathered today to give thanks to God for the gift of Jim's life and we're gathered as well to give thanks to God for the gift of his resurrection, the gift that has us believing that Jim's life has been changed not ended. Jim is now enjoying the resurrected life that Jesus promised. He's there amidst his family and friends who had preceded him in death and my guess is that he's probably fishing now on one of those great Lakes that happen to adorn God's kingdom, downing a few Labatt's Blue with a bag of chips to go with it.

LAMPLIGHTER

Describe as to how they will best be remembered.

In the days prior to electricity, the streets were lit by gas lamps. Each section of the city had somebody designated as the lamplighter and that lamplighter had to go from lamp to lamp, lighting them with a burning torch. One day the famous English author James Ruskin was sitting in his house gazing out his front window. Across the valley was a street on a hillside and Ruskin could see the torch of the lamplighter doing his nightly chores. But because of the darkness and the distance, he could not see the lamplighter, only the torch and the trail of light it left behind. After a short time, Ruskin turned to the person to his right and said: "There's a good illustration of how I would like to be remembered. I'd like to be remembered as someone whom many may have never known, whom people may not have ever seen or met, but they'll know that I passed through their world by the trail of light I left behind."

I don't know if Father Joe ever vocalized as to how he'd like to be remembered, but remembered he will be. He'll be remembered as someone who didn't just talk the talk, but he walked the walk as well. Many people have gone to God, come back to God, or have stayed close to God not so much because of Father Joe's clerical collar but because of the person behind that collar. He embodied care and concern far beyond the prayers he said or the Masses he celebrated or the confessions he heard. If there was someone sick, he was there to visit them. If there was someone in trouble, he was there to bail them out. If there was someone who needed an outlet for their woes, he was there to listen. If there was someone who needed a shoulder to cry on, he was there to supply it. Father Joe didn't just talk about caring for others, he did it. He walked the walk and in doing so, left his mark on many lives.

Father Joe will also be remembered for honesty and humility.

I remember hearing an elderly woman complaining about the fact that that she couldn't drive anymore, and Father Joe barked: "Thank God for that, one less woman driver on the road." Now, admittedly, some of his honesty could be a bit rough, but one thing was for sure, you knew where he stood. He didn't play games. And he'd tell you the truth even though you might not have wanted to hear the truth.

And when it comes to humility, you couldn't find a humbler man than he. There were no airs about him. Although honored as a Monsignor in the Catholic Church, he still preferred to be called Father Joe. He had never to my knowledge owned a new car and never thought himself to be any better than anyone else.

Father Joe will also be remembered for his humor. I wish I had a tape recorder of my conversation with Father Joe when I visited him in the intensive care unit of a hospital this past Saturday. It was vintage Father Joe. He had just been taken off the respirator and the first thing he said to me was: "Those rats! I was finally getting out of this life, and they went and brought me back." Father Joe had me laughing throughout most of our conversation. And that's the way Father Joe would be in most conversations. He'd make remarks, sometimes unfortunately, for those who didn't know him, remarks that took on the appearance of an insult. But that was his mode of operation; he'd say outrageous things all with the intent of generating laughter.

As some of you know, Father Joe was thinking seriously of moving into one of the priest retirement homes. Thank God it didn't happen because he would not have been happy there. It turned out that he was the first one on the list for a room, should there be a vacancy. Telling that story to one of his friends, he concluded the story by saying: "Look, do me a favor, pray that a priest dies." I can't tell you how many times he's come to the Pastoral Care office at Sisters Hospital saying similar outrageous things to the delight and laughter of our staff who came to love him.

Father Joe will also be remembered as a down-to-earth priest. A mantra that was used to describe him at his 50th anniversary of priesthood was a mantra he was proud to own. The mantra went:

"a priestly priest and a manly man. I dare say that there was not a manlier priest in this entire diocese than Father Joe." You'd often see him with his patented T-shirt driving the lawn mower as he cut the grass throughout the church property. You'd see him with his lumberjack shirt plowing the snow in the parking lot. Father Joe was never averse to getting his hands dirty. And he was most at home pounding down a few beers with his friends at a local tavern. It was that down-to-earth quality about him which endeared him to almost everyone he met, and which made him not only one of the most sought-after priests by laypeople across the community, but also made him one of the most popular priests in the diocese.

Father Joe will also be remembered as a "softy" which is hard to believe given his rough and tough exterior and booming voice for which he was famous. At my ordination banquet, my master of ceremonies asked me how he could best describe Father Joe and I told him that if you had an auditorium full of people and could only afford one security guard, he was the man for the job. Well, despite that truth, once you got to know him, you'd find rather quickly that inside that rough and tough exterior lay a soft and caring heart.

I'm afraid that if I did to kids today what Father Joe used to do to them in the parking lot of this parish every Sunday, I would be arrested. Father Joe would boot more than a few of them in the rear end with his shoe. He'd pin back the ears of many of the young boys that walked past him, and being an equal opportunity offender, he'd also pull the hair of the young girls that walked past him. And the funny thing about it was that the kids would get very upset if he didn't do it. You see, the kids knew of the soft heart behind those roughhouse tactics, and they saw those roughhouse tactics as signs of endearment which they were.

And what was true of kids was true of adults as well. I still chuckle about the time I visited a patient at Sisters Hospital who thought the world of Father Joe. When I told her that I'd be seeing him very soon, she said: "Tell him I said hello, tell him when you see him that the person he calls 'woman' sends her best." Of course, as you know, he'd call every one of the female gender "woman" often doing so with a voice that could be heard three blocks away. Now you would suspect that would scare people away from him, but it didn't and that was because they knew of his soft heart.

Father Joe will also be remembered as a hard-working priest. One of the things I used to hate when I was stationed as a deacon in this parish was that Father Joe hardly ever took a vacation and, except for an infrequent morning round of golf, he'd never take a day off. As a result, I never had the luxury of not having him breathing down my neck. This parish was blessed with a man who gave 24/7 to his parishioners, a man who wouldn't dare to be absent when there was a parish function. Father Joe wrote the book on pastoral presence and that was evident by the fact that there's not a person here in this parish who can remember his not being present at the tragic moments, the sad moments, the happy moments, the key moments of their lives.

Father Joe will also be remembered as a father and a mentor to us all. I was talking to the parish trustee the other day and he remarked as to how losing Father Joe was like losing his own father and that's because he was like a father to most of us here today. He founded this parish when a good many of you were nearing the prime of your life and he shaped and molded you to be tireless workers for the church, shaped and molded you to be ambassadors for Christ, shaped and molded you to be a good husband or a good wife or a good father or a good mother.

And Father Joe, as you know, always looked old despite how young he might've been and that gave him the appearance of an Old Sage. And for all intents and purposes, he was a Sage. You could go to him with your problems and go to him with your pains and somehow, he'd say something or do something that may not have made it all better, but it made you feel better, you'd walk away enriched and enlightened.

Speaking from my side of things, Father Joe was a model for a priesthood of integrity and vitality and honor and dedication. And although his model of church differed from mine, there was no questioning his love for people, and it was his love for people that most attracted me to him and has forever served as the bar for priesthood that I have strived to reach.

And finally, Father Joe will be remembered as a true and blue Irishman. For Father Joe, only Easter trumped St. Patrick's Day as the most important religious feast of a calendar year. One of his greatest joys was to march in the St. Patrick's Day parade. He spoke glowingly last Saturday about the top hat he owned which went back to the 19 century, as well as a shillelagh of similar vintage, both of which he would leave to one of his nephews to further the St. Patrick's Day tradition and further his Irish heritage. Father Joe may not of have had the blarney for which many an Irishman is famous, but he had the twinkle in his blue eyes, the love of Irish music and of course the love for the spirits which he could handle better than any Irishman I've ever known.

So, it seems to me that the metaphor James Ruskin used to indicate how he would like to be remembered can be applied to Father Joe. Like that lamplighter on the street in the valley beyond Ruskin's front window, wherever Father Joe went, wherever he worked, he left a trail of light behind. The light of humor and honesty and devotion and love and softness and dedication and inspiration, and that light will continue to shine till the end of time.

The Irish poet W.H. Auden, while standing at the graveside of his friend Yeats on the day of his funeral, said to all who could hear him: "Earth, receive an honored guest!" We say tonight: "Lord God, receive an honored guest and thank you for sharing him with us for over 85 years."

PRESENT IN SPIRIT

Describe in detail as to how despite their death, their presence will be felt.

Back in 1942, when Douglas MacArthur was in command of our troops in the Pacific theater of operation during the Second World War, he wanted to free the Philippines from the grip of the Japanese. After first setting foot on the Island, he needed to retreat hastily as Japan's presence was far greater than he had thought. Before he left, he mouthed that very famous line to the

Filipinos who could hear him. He said distinctly and resolutely, "I shall return!" And return he did; the Japanese were indeed driven from the Island and the people of the Philippines regained their freedom and they were eternally grateful.

This very day in honor of his memory, whenever roll call is taken in the Philippine Army, all names are called and one name is added, and that's the name of Douglas MacArthur. When his name is called, there's an officer designated to respond and that officer shouts: "Present in spirit!"

I reference that Douglas MacArthur story because the truth is that if a roll call is taken in the future at the many and varied places where Bob Conrad lived and worked and played and the name "Bob" is called out, one can honestly and truthfully proclaim "Present in spirit!"

That presence will especially be felt in the kitchen of Bob's home on Whitfield Street. I believe there is a chair in that kitchen where Bob always sat and from that chair Bob would often offer words of wisdom. That chair also put Bob in a position where he could take care of his best friend, the family dog. Three times a day, that dog would be the beneficiary of what Bob called, the three, two, one plan: "three biscuits, two treats and one bone.

That chair also provided Bob with a strategic spot from which he could check out the various young men or women who may have been dating one of his children. If he called you "Bud", be you male or female, you knew you were OK as far as Bob was concerned.

That chair also served as the place where he babysat his children when they were toddlers as he'd warm-up their milk bottles and feed them from the various bottles of baby food his wife Monica had left for him to use. Bob was "Mr. Mom" long before that expression was ever uttered. When it was not fashionable or expected for a husband or father to do so, Bob took charge of the 2 a.m. feedings, the changing of diapers, and the daily baths.

Bob will also be present in spirit at Okell Field when Little League Baseball gets underway this coming spring. One of the great loves of Bob's life was coaching baseball. He held his first practice in the backyard of his home with the kids surrounding a blackboard from which he'd explain what a baseball was, what a baseball mitt happened to be and how a bat was constructed. Once he had them at Okell Field, he'd teach them the basics when it came to batting and fielding and base stealing, and should a player show any fear when it came to their standing at the plate, he would kneel right beside them and talk them through every pitch, calmly dispelling the fear they may have felt and advising them on when to swing and when to get out of the way as a fastball arrived at the plate. Bob touched a lot of lives through the giving of himself in the role of a coach and many a person in this community fondly remembers their playing under his tutelage.

Bob will also be present in spirit on many of the golf courses of this community. He and his brother founded the annual family golf tournament still held to this day, the 40th annual to be held this summer. It was a joy playing golf with Bob because he was always good company and always fun to be with.

Bob will also be present in spirit whenever there are smiles and whenever there is laughter. Bob had a glass eye which became for him a source of hilarity and for the sake of those of you with weak stomachs; I won't go into detail as to how that eye became a source of hilarity. Bob loved to tease, and Bob loved when people enjoyed a good laugh, even if it came at his expense.

So in the months and the years ahead, whenever Mike or Greg or Jack or Karen or Nancy or Joan get together, whenever there is laughter and teasing and good storytelling, whenever there is a feeling of warmth or a feeling of being loved, whenever there are toddlers laughing, whenever there is a sound of the crack of a bat or the ping of a golf ball, take a roll call with the names of the people who are present and then add Bob's name to the list and have someone proclaim loudly and resolutely: "Present in Spirit!"

We're here today to celebrate new life. We believe as Christians that whenever someone dies, they live on. That's the legacy of the cross and the resurrection of our Lord Jesus Christ. Bob may be present with us in spirit, but he's present as well in the resurrected life that Jesus promised and where peace and happiness eternally reign. We believe that he is back together again with many of his family members and friends who preceded him in death. Bob is into eternal life, and it could well be said that heaven is now a better place because he happens to be there.

A CATCHER IN THE RYE

Mention the interventions, the support provided, and the rescues undertaken when friends had gone astray.

Many years ago, in my sophomore year of high school, I read *The Catcher in the Rye* by JD Salinger. I'm suspecting many here read that same book as well. The book is the story of a teenager named Holden Caulfield who flunks out of school and is about to return home to New York City. Before he leaves, one of his teachers asks him about what he plans to do with the rest of his life. Caulfield mulls over the question and then responds to that teacher that he'd like to become a catcher in the rye.

He goes on to explain as to how it's the result of a dream, "a nightmare really," he said, where he is standing at the edge of a cliff. Before him, as he faces away from the deep fall, he sees scores of children wandering aimlessly through a field of rye. The rye has grown so tall that they cannot see where they happen to be heading. Periodically, one or two of them wander too close to the cliff and they fall to their deaths.

"In the dream," said Caufield, "I call to the children to turn back, but many cannot hear me. Not knowing what else to do, I take a stand at the edge of the cliff, and I run and catch as many a kid as I can, rescuing them from a fall that would've most certainly ended their life. I can't catch them all," he said, "but I catch as many as I can, and I wake up. I know it's all a dream," said Caufield to that teacher, "but every time I wake up, I always think to myself that when I grow up, I want to be a catcher in the rye."

I am not sure if Barney ever said or was asked as to what he wanted to be when he grew up, but it seems to me that in talking with those who knew him and reflecting upon the things they said, Barney grew up to become a catcher in the rye. Now, admittedly, there were times when we worried that he was going to fall off a cliff, but in all actuality, Barney spent a good portion of his life making sure his family and his friends never did fall from the edge of any cliff. He spent a good portion of his life making sure that his family and friends had the support and encouragement and the help they needed when they found themselves wandering in rye that had grown so tall that they couldn't see which direction they needed to go.

When Barney discovered that his friend Dan had made the same mistakes with colleagues as he did, he kept Dan focused on what needed to be done and kept on him every step of the way. He did something similar when it came to Joe and Tom. When Barney discovered that any of his friends had a problem or was in trouble in any way, he was right on them. Paul tabbed him as the go-to-guy if any crisis brewed as he could be counted on, he could be relied upon, to drop everything he was doing to help the moment he heard your voice.

Cathy told me how Barney was the go-to-guy whenever kids got into a jam. He'd mentor them, he guided them, he did things Cathy never knew he did. He played a similar role with the kids of many of his friends. It was all part of his keeping them from falling off a cliff.

As someone well said, he was a leader and not a follower, and as a leader he protected everyone he could. In essence, Barney responded to the noblest calling of all: he grew up to become a catcher in the rye.

And when Barney wasn't on watch around the cliffs of life, he'd be found lighting up a room, and he did so, as someone put it, by not saying a word. He had a great sense of humor and enjoyed seeing and making people laugh. Tom told me that the last tweet he got from Barney was just after the scandal that rocked the Penn State football program. He tweeted: "What am I going to do now with my Happy Valley T-shirt?"

Barney was also as genuine a person as you could possibly find and when it came to work, no one worked as hard as he did. To call him a "character" was an understatement. And in reflecting back upon his life, it appears that in his own unique way, Barney made it a point to bring people together.

Barney and I go back to 1980 when he played for the St. Ambrose baseball team. I dug out an old scorebook last night and I saw he played left field and batted second and he even pitched a couple of games. A majority of that team went to the same high school and Barney was the only kid from St. Ambrose who knew the kids from the other neighboring grade schools, and he made it a point to introduce them to the St. Ambrose kids. That would prove to spark a bond amongst them that gave way to friendships still strong and vibrant to this very day.

Barney left life much too soon, but he left his mark. He made an impact. He made a difference. He touched many a heart and many a soul, something often missing from many a dossier of those who lived far more years than he.

It was said by an old Sage that when we are born, we cry, and the world rejoices. He went on to say that we need to live our life in such a way that when we die, the world cries and we rejoice. Barney lived precisely that kind of life. When Barney died, many tears were shed, and they continue to be shed. You could truthfully say the world cried.

At the same time, however, Barney rejoiced. He rejoiced because he entered God's celestial kingdom where peace and happiness eternally reign. We believe as a Christian people that when we die, our life is changed not ended and when the body of earthly dwelling lies in death, we gain an everlasting dwelling place in heaven. Barney has gained that everlasting dwelling place. He's now reunited with all of his loved ones who preceded him in death and there will come a time when we will see him again. In the meantime, we must do our best, in his name, to catch those in the rye from falling from a cliff he or she may have failed to see.

A LAPIDARY ARTIST

Describe their particular skills: the scratches they remedied, the lives they touched, the souls they soothed and the hearts they warmed.

A wealthy ruler possessed a large, unusually brilliant diamond. It was his proudest possession. One day, it accidentally suffered a scratch. Downtrodden and depressed over what had transpired, the wealthy ruler visited lapidary artists hoping that one could remedy the damage, but there wasn't a one capable of such delicate work.

Several months later, a lapidary artist who was also an experienced diamond cutter stepped forward and agreed to remedy the scratch with the assurance that he'd make the stone even more beautiful than it had been before. The wealthy ruler was skeptical at first but then he entrusted him with his precious diamond.

The elderly lapidary artist proceeded to design a beautiful full-blown flower using the scratch as the very stem from which buds, leaves, and a large, gorgeous rose would come forth. He then applied his cutting tools to the diamond and made that design a reality and it was indeed more beautiful than it had been before.

Art was not what you would call a lapidary artist and he had no diamond cutting ability as far as I know; but Art was an artist and an excellent one at that and he often used his talent, his artistic skills, to remedy a scratch, to lighten the loneliness or the sadness or the spirit of someone he happened to encounter along life's way.

Whether it be dollhouses to be auctioned off for a local charity; whether it be tabletop easels for the Alzheimer's Association; whether it be a 3-D re-creation of a 1940s movie set; whether it be a simple flower, a caricature, or golfing trophy; whether it be hand-drawn images of famous people; you're always struck by the details, mesmerized by the design, and captured by the creative mind which happened to lie behind it. And in each and every case, the ultimate recipient of Art's artistic talents could well be likened to that full-blown flower that old lapidary artist drew upon that ruler's precious gem. Art's creations either addressed a scratch that needed to be remedied, a cause that needed to be supported, a life that need to be brightened, uplifted or be filled with peace.

And if Art's artistic skills didn't accomplish that, his writing skills most certainly did. Art expressed a wish early in life to be a writer. He even took a couple of classes on journalism. It never came to pass as his profession but write he did, and he did it well. With his trusty typewriter, he would often roll out "letters to the editor," many of which got featured in the local newspaper. He often wrote these long essays which he'd send to friends and family most of which reflected his philosophy of life. He once wrote that he found great comfort sitting down at his typewriter and typing thoughts that ran through his mind, thoughts resembling a sermon you might hear on a Sunday morning.

He was so good at letter writing that the soldiers in his battalion during the Second World War would often ask him to compose the letters they needed to send home to their loved ones. And so many of the letters that he wrote proved to be sources of consolation and wisdom for their recipients.

And so many of those letters were filled with wonderful quotes. He especially liked the line attributed to Seneca, the famous Native American: "Don't judge anyone till you walked a mile in their moccasins!" And then there was that quote: "If every one of us put our cares and troubles in a huge pile and you could then take your pick of any of those cares and troubles that had been placed there, you'd probably be glad to get back what you placed there." And there was that patented line which read: "Yesterday is gone, tomorrow isn't here yet, and now is the only guarantee we have at the moment."

If you thought Art's paintings were big on detail, so were his writings. He typed an autobiography that could've easily filled more than two hundred pages. Art proved to be as good with his pen and typewriter as he was with his paintbrushes and drawing pencils.

And if his writing skills and artistic skills were not enough to remedy a scratch or support a cause or uplift and brighten a life, there was always Art himself and the way he conducted his life. Art led a life filled with many endearing qualities. There was, first of all, his devotion to his wife Ethel. I think you all know the story about the green carnation. Art worked as a milkman and Ethel's family home was part of his route. And whenever he delivered milk to that home, the residents kept telling him about this pretty girl that lived on Morton Street. On St. Patrick's Day, that pretty girl put a green carnation in an empty milk bottle. Art left a note that he'd pick her up that night and take her to the movies. Five years later they were married and so began a love affair that went on until Ethel died.

What was so striking about that love affair was Art's devotion to Ethel. When Ethel got stricken with Alzheimer's disease and needed placement in a skilled nursing facility, Art was at her side almost daily and it required a 35 mile drive each way. I dare say that a more devoted husband than Art could not be found, and that devotion would prove to be an inspiration to each and everyone who witnessed it.

And Art was a also member of what Tom Brokaw called "The Greatest Generation." The Japanese attacked Pearl Harbor just about the time when Art and Ethel became husband and wife and like so many men of his time, Art was happy to serve his country in the Second World War and did so admirably and courageously. Art rose to the rank of Captain. His good friend Vernon who served with him in the war described Art as the most likable officer you could ever meet and how those under his command always knew that Art had their backs. Like Art's devotion to Ethel, Art's devotion to his country and his service in the Second World War was an inspiration as well to all who witnessed it.

And then there was Art's indomitable spirit. Those positive messages, those positive perspectives found in so many of Art's letters took on flesh in the way Art conducted his life. When Art left Buffalo to take up residence in an assisted living facility in Pittsburgh, Pennsylvania, he did so without batting an eyelash. His mantra throughout his stay at the facility was that one line: "I haven't a thing to complain about." As was true throughout his life, nothing fazed Art. He was accepting of all of life's trials and tribulations. He never let them douse his indomitable spirit.

And then there was Art's charm, the way he could make someone's day by something he said or make someone's day by something he did. Art would make these care packages which included cakes and cookies and other gifts. How he wrapped them was a beauty to behold. And he'd send those care packages to the people he loved to make their day. And when it came to the place where Ethel lived the last years of her life and when it came to the place where Art lived the last years of his life, Art would charm the staff of both facilities commenting on their beautiful eyes or beautiful hair and always affirming the wonderful job they were doing or just complementing them in every way he could. It's no wonder as to how he was the staff's most favorite visitor or the staff's favorite patient.

Besides his charm and positive spirit, besides his inspirational devotion to his wife and country, there's also Art's generosity. His snow blowing his neighbors property, his volunteering for the Alzheimer's Association, his artistic creations for the sake of charity, and his willingness to do whatever he could for his family and his friends and his community. Art was, without question, a giving person. He was generous to a fault, and many were the beneficiaries of his generosity.

And so, like that old lapidary artist who remedied that scratch on that diamond of that wealthy ruler, Art remedied many a scratch he found on a person he encountered along life's way. He did so with his artistic talent, he did so with his writing talent, he did so by his living of a beautiful life, a life that was filled with many endearing qualities. And as was the case with that diamond, the end result was that he or she whose sadness or loneliness or depression he lightened, whose scratch he remedied, whose cause he supported, their lives were enhanced and brightened and given a shot in the arm thanks to what it was that Art had done for them.

We are gathered here today not only to give honor and pay tribute to Art's life, but we are also here to celebrate fact that he's begun new life, a life free of pain and suffering, a life without the physical and mental limitations which aging imposed upon him. Jesus died and rose from the dead to assure us all that when we come to death, life is changed, not ended and when our earthly dwelling lies in death, we gain an everlasting dwelling place in heaven. Art is enjoying once more the company of all those he loved in life. And there will come a time when we will see him again.

GOLDEN CRESCENT HALO

Tell of how they positively influenced many a life, how the "gold" of their inner nature still shines.

If you ever get a chance to visit Eastern Europe, you will come upon many Orthodox churches. And if you make it a point to visit them, you will note as to how the inside walls of a great many are covered with paintings, usually paintings of biblical characters or those of particular saints. What is unique about those paintings is that each character, each saint has a golden crescent halo above their heads. It's one of the hallmarks of Eastern art.

As has happened, the smoke of countless candles lit throughout those churches over its many years has blackened the church's interiors and caused many of the images of those saints and those biblical characters to fade. However, their halo, because of its golden nature, still manages to brightly shine.

When a visitor steps inside one of those churches, all that he or she can see are the halos, and then once their eyes adjust to the darkness, they can dimly make out the faces of the saints and biblical characters present beneath their golden halo.

Now I see that as a metaphor for life. Long after we ourselves have faded away, long after we've died, the gold of our influence will still manage to live on, the golden beam of our inner nature can still be found shining brightly.

Such is the case when it comes to Mary Whelan. She has faded from our sight. God has taken her home, but the gold of her influence still manages to live on, the gold of her inner nature still beams brightly. You can see that in the lives of her children Patrick and Dennis and Kevin and Cathy. Mary was a confidant to them all. It they needed someone to talk to, she was there to listen. If they needed a laugh, she was there to provide it. And if they needed a helping hand, she was there to give it. Mary was the glue that kept the family together, the great buffer in times of turmoil.

At last night's wake, I heard the famous story involving our friend Joe whom as many of you know is not one for tact or discipline. One of Mary's passions was cooking, and Joe happened to arrive while she was in the midst of preparing one of her exquisite meals. One of those large bottles of chili sauce needed to be opened and Joe, sensing that need, decided, against Mary's wishes, to take on the task. Mary's husband arrived on the scene just as the bottle got opened and from head-to-toe Mr. Whelan found himself bathed in chili sauce. If it wasn't for the master reconciler and buffer Mary Whelan, Joe would probably not be with us here today.

Mary was not just a mother to her four children, but she was also a friend who actively looked out for their welfare. The gold of her love still shines through for them. And what Mary was to her children, she also was to her grandchildren. She wasn't only their grandma; she was also their friend. She was someone they could talk to. Sitting with grandma and sharing with her a cup of coffee was a real treat to all of them. The gold of grandma's love shines brightly in the lives of all the grandkids.

And as had been true for the children and grandchildren, so it was with Mary's sister Gertrude. Mary was the oldest sister who always looked after her and that was so, not only in childhood but in adulthood as well. When Gertrude's husband had serious surgery, Mary was there for support, never leaving her sister's side. Mary was not just Gert's sister; she was her best friend. The gold of Mary's love still shines brightly in Gertrude's life.

Such was the case with all of Mary's friends and acquaintances. Mary Whelan has faded from our sight. God has taken her home. But she still lives on, the gold of her halo still shines brightly, and you can see that in the hearts and minds and souls of all who were the recipients of her care, her love, her kindness and her generosity.

And not only does Mary Whelan live on through all of you, but she also lives on in the resurrected life that Jesus promised. In the Gospel I read today; Jesus was getting his disciples ready for the death he would soon experience. He used the symbol of the grain of wheat and how it was necessary for the grain to die for it to become wheat. He was making the point that from death comes forth new life. And if you have any doubts as to that truth, consider your own life and all the deaths you've already undergone as you've evolved into whom you are today.

Though we mourn Mary's death, we are also happy for her new life, a life freed of pain and suffering, a life that will never end. She is now a citizen in God's heavenly kingdom and enjoying a wonderful reunion with all her friends and family who preceded her in death. And as far as her influence is concerned, it still goes on, her halo still shines. Look around you and you'll see that to be true.

A PERSON OF EXCELLENCE

I used this frame only twice. Not many can be likened to a Rossini, not many have set the bar of excellence at a height far beyond anyone's reach.

I believe it was Robert Browning who told a story regarding the renowned composer Giuseppe Verdi. It was opening night for an opera he had just written, and even though it failed to match the high standards employed in his previous operas, Verdi had no qualms about putting it on.

At the end of the performance, he is called onto the stage to accept the wild acclaim of the audience. He knows in his heart that the opera is not as good as it should be, that it's fallen short of being excellent, that it's in desperate need of revision. The audience, however, is excited and noncritical. They are screaming their praise and Verdi is bowing and throwing kisses, basking in the glory of their acclaim.

He then glances up to the balcony box on his immediate left and recognizes the presence of the old operatic master, his old teacher Gioachino Rossini. He is sitting and not standing, his face is expressionless, and his hands are not in the applaud mode, they're folded across his lap.

Verdi turns a shade of red and knows in an instant that he's undeserving of the mindless acclaim of the audience, that he needs to leave the stage immediately and head back to his studio, back to his paper and pen and proceed to vastly improve the opera, to make it expressive of the best of which he was capable, expressive of excellence and nothing short of excellence.

I opened with that anecdote from the world of Opera because, first, I know:

Dr. Bill Bukowski was a lover of the arts, a lover of classical music. I am not sure that he liked Opera, but I suspect that he did. The second reason is because I believe Dr. Bukowski was like a Rossini to many of us. He stood for, he modeled excellence. He represented just about the best there is to be found when it comes to a physician, when it comes to a father and husband, when it comes to a person of faith, when it comes to a human being. And so, whenever we were in his presence, like Giuseppe Verdi in the presence of Rossini, we were reminded of what excellence is all about and how much farther we might need to go to realize it.

I happen to be one of Dr. Bukowski's ex-patients and I chose him as my physician because I was enamored of his dedication to his patients, his calm and deliberate manner, and just the overall wonderful way in which he conducted his craft. The problem, however, was that I had a hard time facing him when I knew that I didn't do what he asked me to do. He'd tell me that I needed to lose a few pounds and, when I'd come to my next visit a few pounds heavier, he'd never scold me or reprimand me but he gave me that look, like the one Rossini gave to Verdi, and I knew right away that my excuses for gaining weight were lame and the fact of the matter was that I wasn't disciplined enough, I didn't try hard enough to do what he knew to be in my best interest to do.

I can't tell you the number of times I cancelled my appointment in the hopes that by that newly scheduled time I'd rise to the occasion and lose the weight I was perfectly capable of losing if I put my mind to it. And the funny thing is that I'd lose the weight, not so much for my own sake, but for the fact that I so respected the man that I didn't want to let him down.

In talking to Barbara, Kate, Beth, Martha, Peter, Bill, and Joan, I have a suspicion that the same kind of dynamics went on with them. Since all of their physical needs were met, since they were blessed, Dr. Bukowski expected them to give of themselves, to pay back to the community from the blessings they were given. I'm sure they do that, I'm sure they've done that because they so respected their dad that in no way did they want to let him down.

Now that kind of respect is only afforded to Rossini type individuals, individuals of impeccable integrity, individuals who stand out from the crowd, individuals whom you stand up for when they come into a room because you see in them the kind of qualities that speak of all that is grand and noble and exemplary in life.

Think, if you will, of Bill Bukowski, the physician. At one time, the man had 1400 patients and all of them would always receive his individual attention. His clinical skills were of such high caliber that he was the doctor's doctor at Sisters Hospital. He took one day off every other week, that's how dedicated he was to his patients and his profession and whether it be in the middle of dinner or 4 a.m. in the morning, he'd respond to a call and never once showed any displeasure. He was a perfect gentleman, always dapper with his bowtie, and he coolly and calmly handled any emergency, and never once did he fail to respect and nurture the nurses and healthcare professionals who worked alongside him. You had in Dr. William Bukowski the finest qualities a physician could possibly have.

Think, if you will, of Bill Bukowski the man. First, he was a man of strong faith. When he worked regularly at Sisters Hospital, he made more trips to the chapel than I did. This faith was more than just in his heart; it was on his sleeve as well. When I inquired of Dr. Daniel McCue of any anecdotes in regard to Dr. Bukowski, he said: "He was so straight laced, so much a man of impeccable character, that there were no anecdotes!" Dr. Bukowski was about as Christ-like a man that you'd ever find. Dr. John Lore probably said it all when he said: "If Bill Bukowski is not in heaven, then none of us have a chance!"

Bill Bukowski was also a man of strong virtue. He not only shined forth with elegance and integrity, but he modeled unselfishness as well. He was always extending himself whenever there was a need and he always made sure that other's needs were met before his own. He was also someone whom I don't believe ever said a bad word. One time, he had just finished getting his basement remodeled. A new ceiling and a new rug had been installed. Unbeknownst to him, the toilet on the first floor began to overflow and the water leaked through to the basement staining both that ceiling and that rug. When he discovered what had happened, the worst that came out of his mouth was: "Oh! Dear!" Someone described him as the only man they knew whom everybody liked.

And then how about the virtues he modeled in the last two years of his life? When Bill was inflicted with ALS, Lou Gehrig's disease, he put his best foot forward and made the best of what have had to have been a horrible set of circumstances. Those of you who were as privileged as I was to be at the Buffalo Club this spring when Dr. Bukowski received his "Man of the Year Award," we witnessed a moment of great courage and humility. He came to the podium, and with his computer and its speaker, he typed out words of thanks: "Thanks for the privilege of working at Sisters Hospital, thanks for all that Sister's had done for him." The kids will tell you about how, when aides would come to the house, he was never without a thank you, never without a show of dignity. As much as Dr. Bukowski stood out from the crowd during his days of health, he stood out even further in his days of sickness.

Dr. William Bukowski, the doctor, the father, the husband, the person of faith, the man! He was a giant in all those categories. He modeled excellence in all the phases of his life. He modeled just about the best you'll ever see when it comes to the living of a life.

My friends, as Rossini was to Verdi, so was Dr. Bill Bukowski to so many of us. His presence reminded us all of what we should be striving for in life. May our love, our respect, our admiration for this man propels us to be people of integrity, of courage, of dedication, of virtue, and of goodwill. In that way Dr. William Bukowski, who lives now in eternal life with God, can also live on in us. I'm going to stop now. I think that Dr. Bukowski is probably pretty upset that I made such a big deal of his life.

MISSING BUT NOT GONE

Draw a blueprint of their life and tell of how we'd best mourn their absence by working off that blueprint and incorporating a "best" attribute or two into the way we conduct our life.

A lady on a train reported to the conductor that, since she boarded the vehicle, her purse had been stolen from her handbag. A fruitless search was conducted, and warnings went out to the other passengers to be on high alert. Ne'er-do-wells were questioned. Suddenly, with great apology, the lady who reported the stolen purse tells of her finding it. It happened to be her birthday and her daughter that morning had gifted her with a new handbag that had multiple compartments and she discovered her missing purse in one of the compartments of the handbag that had eluded her attention.

I'm reminded here of the old gentleman who searched everywhere for the spectacles which happened to have been lying across his brow. Or the clerk who ransacked his desk in search of the pencil that sat behind his ear. Or the schoolboy who charges his brother with the theft of his pen knife which lurked in the depths of a pocket he had only haphazardly searched.

Death is like that purse and those spectacles. Death is like that pencil and that pen knife. It has us believing that the person we loved is gone. It has us believing that the person whom we cherished has disappeared from our sight. But the truth is, the fact is that the person that we loved and cherished isn't really gone, the person that we loved and cherished has not disappeared from our sight. They happen to be on our person, they happen to be embedded in our heart and mind and soul.

Rabbi Sam Porath once said that when those we loved have died, they'd like nothing more than to be granted a curtain call, another appearance upon the stage of life. And we grant them that curtain call, we grant them that appearance when the best qualities of their life can be seen in us, when those who knew and loved them can't help but notice how they're living on in us.

So, in this time when we are mourning Pam's death, when we are gathered here saddened by her loss, we have our work cut out for us, we have homework to do. Pam would like that curtain call; she'd like another appearance on the stage of life. She'd like to be found living on in us. And to make that happen, to make that a reality, she's given us a blueprint to follow, the blueprint that was her life.

On that blueprint, you'll find such qualities and traits as being a consummate professional, a loving and caring wife, a terrific mom. On that blueprint, you'll find examples of how she made everyone better just by being in her presence, how she'd give the shirt off her back for whatever cause she got involved in.

On that blueprint, you'll find examples of how she looked out for other people, how she had earned everyone's respect, how she would do anything for anybody, how she found humor in almost anything and how she made us smile with her wicked laugh.

So, my friends, with the blueprint Pam has given us to follow, a blueprint of a life well lived, and a life well loved, we can progress ahead with our homework assignments. We can proceed ahead in granting Pam's wish for a curtain call.

Because, you see, if we could strive to be more professional, if we could strive to be a better husband or a better wife, a better mother or a better father; if we could learn not to take ourselves too seriously, if we can laugh more and be more generous, if we could make it a point to look out for other people; then Pam will get her curtain call, she'll reappear on the stage of life. And that's because people will see her in us, people will see her living on in us.

And she'll live on not only in us but also in the resurrected life that Jesus promised. Jesus let us know that when we die, life is changed and not ended, that when our earthly body lies in death, we gain an everlasting dwelling place in heaven. Pam is in that place of which the Holy Spirit said: "Eye has not seen, nor ear heard what the Lord has prepared for those who have loved him!" Pam has been reunited with all of her friends and family who preceded her in death and there will come a time when we will see her again.

THERE IS ANOTHER PLACE

Tragic though their death may be, tell of the comfort that can be found, the good that can be salvaged.

No other picture captured the tragedy and the heartbreak of the Oklahoma City bombing than that of a firefighter caring a little baby girl away from the rubble of that bombed out building. The day before the bombing, the little girl celebrated her first birthday, the only one she would ever celebrate. Her mother, fighting through her indescribable grief, spoke through her tears and said this: "The only way I can make it, the only thing that keeps me going is that I know she is in heaven now with God and God will take care of her."

The great writer Henry Van Dyke once told of standing on the seashore. He spots a ship spreading her white sails to the morning breeze heading out into the deep blue sea. He watches until the ship hangs like a speck of a white cloud just where the sea and the sky come down to mingle with each other. Then, in a matter of moments, he hears someone shout: "There she goes!"

As Van Dyke saw it, the ship was gone from sight but that was all. The ship was just as large in mast and hull, just as able to bear its living freight as it had been when it left the harbor. And he was sure that it would only be a matter of time when other eyes will see her sailing toward their harbor and when that happens, someone will shout: "There she comes!"

In these times when there are no words to say that make any sense; in these times when our hearts ache and the grief stings; there's consolation in the fact that this is not the only world, that there is a place where the broken things are mended, the wrong is made right and the good does not give way to the bad.

Lynn is in that place. Although the ship of death came to the Otwell home a few days ago, the fact was that God captained that ship and God sailed that ship to the shores of heaven and as they neared those shores, Lynn heard her mom, and many others shout: "There she comes!"

Though Lynn is in a place where there is no more suffering or pain; although everything is now alright with Lynn, everything is not alright with us. We don't know how we're going to manage life without her. We don't know how we're going to carry on our lives without her.

I'm reminded of that story involving Sir Edwin Landseer. He was a painter of large murals, the most famous of which sits upon a wall of a tavern in Scotland. On the day when that mural was dedicated, a bottle of champagne exploded, and its contents sprayed upon the mural causing some of the paint to run. So right in the middle of this beautiful mural, a black stain appeared. Many considered it ruined.

When the last guest left the dedication, Sir Edwin went down to the cellar and retrieved all the paints he had used to create the mural. He then proceeded to paint a waterfall making the stain the bedrock upon which its waters fell. He made other changes in the mural so much so that it looked more magnificent than the original. The stain which could've ruined a beautiful painting would end up adding to the painting's magnificence.

Lynn's death left a dark stain upon all of our hearts and that stain will never go away. But Lynn, however, has left behind a lot of paint for us to use to make something of that stain, the paint being the virtues she beautifully exemplified especially during the course of her battle with cancer.

The virtue of courage stands out. Lynn wasn't just afflicted with one cancer, but dealt with a variety of them, each coming at different times throughout the course of her life. At each juncture, at each attack of cancer, Lynn was bound and determined to defeat it and would then courageously endure the ravages of chemotherapy to make that happen. And always throughout it all, she made sure that it didn't dampen her spirits.

Alongside the virtue of courage stood the virtue of family love wonderfully exhibited till the day she died. Family was everything to Lynn and despite her multiple bouts with cancer, she found the time and the strength to carry on her role as a parent and did a terrific job when it came to the raising of her children. As the end drew near, she found great consolation in having lived long enough to participate in all their weddings. In talking with her a few short weeks ago, the biggest regret as she faced death was her inability to live long enough to witness the birth of her grandchildren.

And besides her being a terrific mother, she was also a great wife to Jim, and they made the best of their times together. And as far as her siblings are concerned, Lynn was their "goal setter", being the first to drive a car, the first to get a degree, the first to get married. Lynn paved the roads for her siblings to travel upon. She proved to be the rock for both the Otwell family as well as the Manley family. She was the glue that kept them all together; the one who pulled the strings necessary for success to be realized.

Also in Lynn's cellar, there was the virtue of her knowing how to have a good time, to make the best of life, to make sure that when life was over, there'd be no regrets. Although that would sometimes translate into Amazon realizing record-setting profits, although that would mean having a UPS truck stop by the house several times in a given day, although that would sometimes mean too many glasses of chardonnay; Lynn lived life to the fullest. She got to travel all over the world, and she never let a minute of life go by without squeezing some sort of enjoyment out of it. Lynn never let her cancer stand in the way of her making the best of her life.

Also in Lynn's cellar, there were the paint cans of the virtues labeled compassion, generosity, the willingness to listen, a love for others, and a care for those she knew and loved.

So, when it comes to that stain Lynn's death left upon our hearts, she's left behind a lot of paint for us to use to make something of the stain. So if we can strive to be more courageous, to not cave in to despair and self-pity when bad things come our way; if we can strive to be more family centered and more family oriented and make sure our family's needs trump our own; if we can strive to make the best of life and live it to the fullest; if we could strive to love more and be more compassionate and more willing to listen and more willing to care; we will not only make something beautiful out of that stain upon our hearts, but we'll also pay Lynn the best tribute we could possibly pay her and build for her the best Memorial we could possibly build. And that would be our allowing her to be seen living on through us, our exhibiting that a lot of Lynn had rubbed off on us.

A few short days ago we celebrated Easter, we celebrated Jesus rising from the dead and, with that rising, came the promise that when we die life is changed not ended and when the body of earthly dwelling lies in death, we gain an everlasting dwelling place in heaven. We're not only celebrating Lynn's life here today, but also celebrating the fact that though she may be gone for a time, that time will not be forever.

THE DEATH OF A TREE

Tell of the people, the places, the communities, the organizations that will feel a great loss. Review the ways and means by which their life will continue on.

Whenever a large, stately or majestic tree dies and is cut down, it is very noticeable. An open space appears where at one time a lot of activity had taken place. Its absence comes as a great loss to many people.

It comes as a great loss to the farmer who had counted on that tree for needed shade for the particular crops he had planted. It comes as a great loss to the artist who had used that tree as a backdrop for many of her paintings. It comes as a great loss to the traveler who had often sought out that tree for some relief from a burning sun. It comes as a great loss to the children who housed their clubhouse on one of its branches and from another hung a swing. Birds and squirrels feel a great loss because many a nest was housed in that tree's nooks and crannies and many a cache of food was stored there for the cold winter months to come.

Whenever a large and stately and majestic tree dies and gets cut down, a lot feel sad, a great many feel a great sense of loss. The good news, however, is that after that tree's remains get sent to the lumber yard, it comes back to life again, it manages to live on.

You see, builders and manufacturers and artist and carpenters will go to that lumber yard and from the dead wood of that tree will come objects of great use and great delight, especially to those who had mourned its absence.

Objects like handles on those tools the farmer needed to care for his plantings or the clapboards he needed for that barn he happened to be building; Objects like Lincoln Logs or baseball bats or skateboards which children will buy to entertain themselves for hours on end.

From the dead wood of that tree will come objects like that exquisite piece of art, compliments of an artist's carvings or that wooden shelter built for weary travelers. From the dead wood of that tree will come objects like a bird house or a feeding station built to the delight of birds and squirrels and other assorted members of the animal kingdom. When a large and stately and majestic tree dies and gets cut down, it comes back to life again, it manages to live on, and much consolation is provided for those who mourned its absence.

Jerry Leibring is gone; a great void has entered many a life, a big loss is felt by many. Coz feels a great loss. The two of them met at high school and they liked each other, but there wasn't more to it than that. But when Jerry went to Vietnam, he wrote to her. (What Coz didn't know was that he wrote to many people.) Coz was told by her mom to write back. And so she did and a budding romance began. And when he was back from Vietnam, that romance subsequently led to marriage. They made it to 50 years. This past year, despite his illness, they had a grand celebration. Coz will miss him dearly.

Eric and Danielle, Jerry's children, they feel a great loss because Jerry was a fantastic father and he loved them very much. James, Sarah, Hannah, and Julia, Jerry's grandchildren, feel a great loss as well, as Grandpa Do, as they called him, made them all feel special, and they each felt the depths of his love.

Jerry's nieces and nephews feel a great loss because, UJ, as some called him, was a joy to be around. They especially cherished his million-dollar smile and were enthralled at his uncanny skills as a euchre player.

Jerry's nurse at Roswell, she also feels a great loss, because Jerry always had a joke for her and found him to be one of the most pleasant and kindest of patients which she had the privilege to take care of.

Jerry's many friends, they feel a great loss. They'll miss his "chats" which Jerry called his favorite pastime. They will miss his patented smile. His hunting friends will especially miss him at this time of the year, prime hunting season, because he was fun to have around, and he was great company.

Jerry, as many of you know, was not a complicated person. He enjoyed the simple pleasures of life. He was easy to get along with and he didn't need much to enjoy life. Nothing pleased him more than to be outside, basking in nature's glory.

And Jerry was a giving person. He gave of himself to our country and earned a Bronze Star for his efforts. He gave of his time for the sake of our environment as he made it a habit to plant as many trees as he could for the sake of the generations that would follow him. Jerry gave of himself for the sake of his family, for the sake of anyone who looked to him for help.

Jerry has died, many are feeling a great loss, a big void has entered many a heart, many are missing him, and many are mourning his loss. But like that tree that died and was sorely missed, like that tree whose loss was mourned by many, it's not going to be the last we'll see of Jerry. His life is not over. His life continues on.

It continues on in a world where peace and happiness eternally reigns, where pain and suffering and sorrow is no more, place of which the Holy Spirit said: "Eye has not seen, nor ear heard, nor has it entered the hearts of people to know what the Lord has prepared for those who loved him." And in that place, he will meet up with all who preceded him in death.

Jerry's life also continues on in our memories and those memories will stay with us until the day when we join him in death. Jerry's life also continues on in all the places that Jerry frequented, all those places where Jerry left his mark. And most especially Jerry's life continues on in all those whom he loved in life; they will forever bear the imprint of his love.

God used Jerry's life when he walked amongst us. God used it to better this world. May we make it a point to carry on for Jerry and in his name help better this world. In our so doing, we'll not only further his legacy but we'll also make sure that he will never be forgotten.

WINSTON CHURCHILL'S FUNERAL

Tell of the chapters to be written and the responses to reveille that will be forthcoming despite their death.

Winston Churchill planned his own funeral. Included in it were some of the great hymns of the Anglican Church and all the particulars of an Anglican liturgy. There were two things that he specifically requested at the end of the liturgy that made the funeral unforgettable to all who had attended.

At the conclusion of the final prayers, silence fell over the packed Cathedral. A bugler, high up in the dome of St. Paul's, began to play the familiar tune of taps. Those haunting notes brought home to everyone the realization that an era had come to an end, a great man was no more, and it was reported that there wasn't a dry eye in the house.

As the last note of taps rang through the Cathedral, another bugler, as Churchill requested, another bugler on the opposite side of the dome began to play reveille: "It's time to get up, it's time to get up, it's time to get up in the morning."

That final touch caught everyone by surprise. A smile replaced tears and it brought home a truth which Churchill firmly believed. The truth that the worst things are never the last things, the truth that reveille and not taps has the final say, the truth that death brings forth new life.

We're here today to celebrate the fact that as hard, and as painful and as devastating as was the loss of our friend Carol, her life is not over. Her life has not come to an end. There are other chapters yet to be written, there are still responses to reveille that will yet be forthcoming.

Some of that, of course, will be taking place in Carol's new residence, God's celestial kingdom, where peace and happiness eternally reigns. I would guess that God's probably got her involved in a great deal of things. But the bulk of those chapters to be written and those responses to reveille that are forthcoming are going to depend on us. We are going to have to pick up where Carol's earthly life left off; we are going to have to carry on for her all the wonderful qualities of living we had seen in her.

And as we all know, there were many. First of all, Carol was a family person through and through. She loved her nieces and nephews as though they were her own. She attended all their sporting events, recitals, birthday parties, you name it, be it any significant event in their life, she was there.

And then you have her extended family, which is all of us here at Sisters Hospital. You weren't a colleague of Carol, you were a sister or a brother to Carol and, in some cases, you were a daughter or son to Carol.

She would mother you if she thought you needed it. She'd be a confidant if you had issues outside of work. She'd be a motivator if she thought you needed a little push or needed a little lift. She'd be your cheerleader if she thought you were doing a good job. She'd be your champion if she thought you were being slighted or overlooked. Carol would provide the shoulder you needed to cry on, and she would be the ear you needed to hear your woes. And most especially, Carol would be a source of compassion and sensitivity and encouragement when you needed it the most.

Another thing about Carol was her competence, her vision, her excellence, her passion especially when it came to her work. Her skills sets were multiple and that made her one of the most valuable members of the Sisters Hospital team. She knew how to balance all the facets of the Catholic Health World. And she could always be counted on for coming up with ideas that no one had ever thought of as well as the little things that many had forgotten. She had a depth of knowledge that few possessed. And when it came to the lab, Carol was its staunchest defender and its greatest champion.

And Carol also exhibited tremendous courage especially when it came to her battle with cancer, when it came to speaking the truth that no one wanted to hear. It would be Carol who would encourage you to show courage especially when it came to your doing something you feared you couldn't do. And you'd be hard-pressed to find anyone with the demeanor and temperament Carol possessed which made her not only approachable but someone who could be counted on to be fair and trustworthy and kind. And there was always that laugh that would serve to melt down whatever tension may have been filling the room. And as far as mentoring goes, there was no better mentor than Carol.

And so, my friends, if we could strive to be more courageous, if we could be as passionate about our work as she was with hers, if we can encourage people more and be more compassionate and less serious, if we could be more family-oriented, if we could be a better cheerleader, a better motivator, a better confidant, if we could display excellence in our work, if we could be as good a mentor as Carol was; if we could do all of that, then we will be adding chapters to Carol's life. We will, in Carol's honor, be responding to that call of reveille.

When we end this service, when we complete this celebration of Carol's life, you will not hear one bugler playing taps and another bugler playing reveille, but the same truth that Winston Churchill tried to relay through those buglers happens to be a truth we hold dear.

We, too, believe that reveille and not taps has the final say. We, too, believe that death brings forth new life. We, too, believe that Carol's life did not come to an end. We believe that she is enjoying the resurrected life that Jesus promised. She is now free of all the pain and suffering that ravaged the end of her life. She is now enjoying a reunion with all the loved ones of hers who preceded her in death.

If we add those chapters to Carol's life, if we do, in Carol's honor, respond to the call of reveille, she will also enjoy living on in each and every one of us.

THE MAN WITH THE GOLDEN KEY

Give examples of the doors he or she may have unlocked.

In his autobiography, G. K. Chesterton, the great author and poet, told of his father. In his childhood, Chesterton had a cherished possession, a toy theater with characters made of cardboard cutouts and a stage and a curtain and assorted stage paraphernalia. One of the characters was this man with the golden key. Chesterton says that he had long since forgotten what that cutout character stood for, but in his mind, that man with the golden key would always be associated with his father because his father unlocked the door for him to see and do so many things.

When I look at the life of Dr. Eustace Phillies, I can't help but conclude that Dr. Phillies was a lot like G. K. Chesterton's father. He was an unlocker of doors for many who got to know and love him; he was the man with the golden key.

First and foremost, he unlocked the door of hematology. Dr. Phillies was on the ground floor in making that brand of medicine the outstanding discipline, the vital cog in the wheel of medical treatment that it happens to be today. He's regarded as one of Buffalo's first hematologists. Although very few knew it, he was recognized internationally for his work in that field. His two sons George and Gregory should be eternally grateful that he chose the hematology field because, you see, his interest in that area of medicine had him looking at blood smears and samples under the microscopes of the hospital lab. That's where he met their mom. He would marry her, and they spent many happy years together.

Dr. Phillies also unlocked the door to financial help for hemophiliacs. From the very beginning of his practice, he looked out for the minority community. He helped a goodly number of ethnic groups who had no means available to pay him. He was especially beloved in the Greek community. He was known fondly amongst his colleagues as the poor man's hematologist.

He was particularly a champion of hemophiliacs who for years were denied the medical benefits which the rest of the community received. Thanks to Dr. Phillies' advocacy and hard work and effort, hemophiliacs today have access to third-party payments for all their medical needs.

Dr. Phillies also unlocked the door of medicine for many people. He was an instructor in the residency as well as nursing programs at Sisters Hospital. He was also associated with the residency training programs at the University of Buffalo where he particularly looked out for non-American aspirants to the medical profession. He was a father figure to many of them, often going out of his way to make them feel welcomed and at home.

Dr. Phillies also unlocked many doors for the arts community. In his own quiet way, Dr. Phillies financially supported many causes that have helped make music and theater and the arts a vibrant part of life in the Western New York Community. He was a true Renaissance man. He not only loved the arts, but he loved history and was well read and knowledgeable in both areas. He was a true promoter of all that is beautiful in life.

But probably the one thing that really stood out in his life was the way he cared for and helped the many sick people who were fortunate enough to have crossed his path. For thousands of people, Dr. Phillies unlocked the door of healing.

When I mentioned Dr. Phillies' name to a friend of mine, he said he was the kindest man he never met. I echo that same sentiment. His kindness, his compassion, his gentleness, his patience did more to help heal patients than many of the pills he happened to distribute or the prescriptions he happened to write. People loved him as a doctor, and he loved them as a patient. To the thousands of Western New Yorkers who were the recipients of his God-given gift of healing, he will be long remembered as someone special.

I could go on with further revelations of this beautiful man but he'd want me to be short and he's probably already embarrassed by the all the attention I've given him. Suffice it to say, for a large number of people, Dr. Phillies was like GK Chesterton's father. He was the man with the golden key. He unlocked many a door during the course of his lifetime.

We gather here today to say goodbye and pay tribute to a wonderful man. We're also here to celebrate his new life. Jesus on the cross unlocked the door of death, so whenever someone dies that life doesn't end, it continues on. Dr. Eustace Phillies now enjoys his eternal reward and there will come a time when we will see him again and enjoy his love.

So, thank you Lord for a wonderful human being, an outstanding gentleman, a true healer, and for all the giving and the sacrifices and the loving that marked his seventy nine years of life. But most especially Lord, thank you for the privilege of having his life touch ours.

FLOWERS

Tell of how he or she brightened many a life, mention the institutions, the places, the individuals that were enamored by their presence.

Famed preacher Leslie Weatherhead once told the story of a boy who was sent by his father to get some seeds from the hardware store, seeds to be used to brighten the yard with flowers. The young lad put some of the seed in a bag and some of the seed in his pocket not realizing that there was a hole in both the pocket as well as the bag. So long as he kept moving it was fine, but if he stopped for any length of time, some of the seed would trickle out and fall upon the ground below. And in his walk home, he stopped quite often.

He stopped at the bridge to see if the creek was rising. And not far from there, he stopped again to greet a farmer friend with whom he had a delightful conversation. And when he passed by the sycamore tree, he stopped there to admire its beauty. And then finally, he walked home. The following spring, beautiful flowers came to be found at all those places where the young lad had stopped.

Commenting on that story, Leslie Weatherhead remarked as to how that paralleled the life that Jesus led because, he said, everywhere that Jesus stopped, beautiful flowers came to be found.

I'm reminded of the two contrasting tombstones in a country cemetery. One adorned the grave of a General who had served in the Second World War. It was a large imposing tombstone. It listed all of the battles and accomplishments that had marked his military career. The other tombstone was far less imposing. It adorned the grave of a twenty-one-year-old woman. It listed no accomplishments of any great renown. It listed but a single sentence. But that sentence spoke more as to the greatness of that life than did the accomplishments and achievements of that General. The sentence on that tombstone read: "Everywhere she went, she brought flowers."

I believe it could be said of Tom Donovan that everywhere he stopped, beautiful flowers came to be found and everywhere that Tom went he, too, brought flowers. Now, of course, we're not talking flowers in the literal sense of that term, but flowers in the sense of the joy he imparted; the beauty he gave rise to; the good things he accomplished; the lives he had brightened; the laughter that he generated; the kindness he showed; the virtues he exemplified. Be it where Tom went, be it where he stopped; the lives and the places and the institutions, they were enriched beyond measure. Be it where Tom went, or where Tom stopped, the encounter would generate a smile.

A prime example came some 43 years ago, when Father Stanton and I came to St. Ambrose Church for the first time. Who can forget that Bicentennial weekend when Father Stanton ran up and down the main aisle preaching like a man on fire and where I dubbed the two of us as the new kids on the block. July and August of 1976 were crazy and hectic days as Father Stanton used the parish council to generate and implement many changes, changes that were needed to bring the parish back to life again.

Tom played a key part in those changes. If my memory serves me correctly, he would follow John Cleary as President of the Parish Council and I remember how he always kept an empty seat at the table for Jesus. Be it Tom's charisma or Irish Blarney, Tom was instrumental in helping the parish through those chaotic times. If it wasn't for the flowers he brought to those parish council meetings, I am not sure the parish would've moved forward and progressed at the speed and in the depths in which it did. St. Ambrose church was enriched beyond measure, thanks to those flowers Tom brought when he appeared on the premises.

And so it went as well with the various taverns that comprised the route for beer deliveries back in the day when Tom drove a beer truck for Gohr Distributors. Tom wasn't one to just drop off beer at the various taverns on his route, he made it a point to get to know his customers and it got to where those customers came to enjoy his presence whenever he arrived for a delivery. Tom was a hard guy not to like. So, between the stories he told and his genuine interest in their welfare, tavern owners always found him a welcomed sight. It could well be said that Tom brought flowers every time he made a tavern stop and tavern owners throughout his route would testify as to how enriched they felt and how much brighter was their day thanks to Tom's having been there.

And then how about those flowers Tom brought to the many loves of his life? I forgot to ask Mary as to how she met Tom, but it could well be said that the two of them struck gold when they met each other. Their love for each other never wavered and their love for each other continued for 61 years. I had the privilege of renewing their vows when they celebrated their 60th anniversary. Mary, I am sure, would testify as to how her life was enriched having Tom as her husband. That her life grew better and brighter and became more colorful than it had been before thanks to the flowers Tom brought into their relationship.

How the two of them managed seven children is beyond me, but they did it and they did it well, they did a fantastic job of parenting. It could well be said that the seven daughters received flowers from Tom every time he saw them. He tabbed each one his favorite, each one felt loved; each one had a unique relationship with their dad. Whenever Tom met with his daughters, it always resulted in their feeling enriched, their feeling better and brighter than they had been before.

And when it came to Tom's eleven grandchildren and four great-grandchildren, flowers came their way as well, compliments of Grandpa. Just as he made each of his daughters feel that they were his favorite, so he made each and every grandchild and great-grandchild feel as though they were his favorite. He had individual conversations with each one of them as he celebrated their victories and cried with them over their defeats. Tom established a bond with every one of them, and as was the case with Mary and the seven daughters; having Tom around brightened their day and enriched their life.

And flowers went out as well when it came to his children's spouses. Having Tom around brightened their day and enriched their lives as well. They were his sons and not sons-in-law and he always left them smiling and left them basking in delight as he'd repeat his classic line: "Proud to know you!" This past Father's Day was a tearjerker for the entire Donovan family as Tom let it be known as to how proud he was to have the special family that he had. To call Tom a family man was a huge understatement.

And also, when you think of it, everyone who had struck a friendship with Tom, they too received flowers as well. Be it his Friday morning coffee buddies; his lifelong friends; the nurses that took care of him at Mercy Hospital; be it yours truly; we all left our encounters with him wearing a big smile and feeling better and brighter than we had been before. We were all enriched beyond measure by having called Tom our friend.

Tom as you know was a storyteller and a first-class raconteur. I'll never forget the story he told how when Mary was at Mercy Hospital for minor surgery, he heard his name get called and when he went to the desk in response, they took him to a back room and had him strip off his clothes and put on a gown. Tom says to himself: "This is great, they're going to take me to the recovery room to see Mary." When they came to get him, he wasn't getting taken to the recovery room, but was getting taken to a surgery suite where colonoscopies were conducted. They thought he was a different Tom Donovan and boy did the Mercy personnel have egg on their face when they realized they had the wrong Tom Donovan. Tom couldn't have laughed harder; he took it all in stride.

So when all is said and done, when you're in the midst of something beautiful, when you're in the midst of laughter and joy and kindness, when you see virtue being exemplified, when you're day is brightened and you feel enriched beyond measure, think of those flowers Tom brought to every place where he happened to stop. Think of the flowers Tom brought everywhere he went. And give thanks to God that you were on the receiving end of those flowers. Give thanks to God as to how enriched your life has been and how privileged you were that those flowers came your way compliments of a man you had come to know and love.

And give thanks to God as well as for the fact that Tom is now in a place where flowers abound, a place where pain and suffering is no more, a place where peace and happiness eternally reigns. Jesus died and rose to assure us all that when we die, life is changed and not ended and when the body of our earthly dwelling lies in death, we gain an everlasting dwelling place in heaven. Tom is probably talking Father Stanton's ear off as we speak and let's hope that those who preceded him in death can get a word in edgewise once he sees them.

BROKEN MIRROR

Tell of the ways he or she shined light into darkened corners, into places where light had never shined.

Alexander Papaderos opened a monastery and established a Peace Center in a city near the coast of Greece. When he was a small boy, Papaderos came upon broken pieces of a mirror next to a motorcycle that had crashed and sat abandoned at the side of a road near the small village in which he lived.

He spent hours trying to put the mirror back together again, but to no avail. So, he decided to take the biggest piece of the broken mirror and rub it against a rock until it was smooth and round. Then he began using it to shine the sun's light into cracks and crevices that had never seen light before. He did that quite often; it became a way for him to pass the time.

113

Many years later, Papaderos, now a young adult, put that rounded piece from a broken mirror in his wallet and kept it there as a reminder, a reminder of what he ought to do with the rest of his life. From that day forward, propelled by that reminder, Alexander Papaderos would become famous. He became famous for doing things and creating things that have served to bring light to the darkened corners of life, famous for shining light where light had never shined before.

Now I don't believe that Marie had a piece from a broken mirror in her purse, but if you look at her life, if you look at the way she conducted herself, I believe you'd agree that she spent a lot of time doing as Papaderos had done, reflecting the sun wherever she went, brightening and uplifting many a sun starved life, reflecting the sun's rays into cracks and crevices spawned by the trials and tribulations of life. Like Papaderos, it became her life's work.

That would clearly be seen in her younger years when she walked the streets with a baby carriage. There was nary a house where she didn't stop, nary a house where she didn't greet the occupant on the porch, always flashing that million-dollar smile. Wherever she went, she was always a welcomed sight. It got to where she knew which neighbors were doing well and which were not and so you'd find her spending a bit more time at the porch of the neighbor who needed someone to brighten their day.

And you would find her doing similar work as a volunteer at the front desk at Deaconess Hospital. Deaconess happened to house many in a terribly debilitated state, and many a visitor would arrive in a sun starved state for they knew that the loved one they were visiting would never leave that facility and would never see a better day. Marie always did her best to try to brighten their day.

It was no accident when Marie came to homes with a high level of distress. She always knew the right things to say, and she'd always manage to deflect the sun's rays into the cracks and crevices that were feeding their distress.

And what Marie did for neighbors and friends and acquaintances, what Marie did for those visitors at Deaconess

Hospital, she also did for her family. Her beloved John undertook the challenge of teaching her how to drive and though it tried his patience and caused a few vulgar words to pass from his lips, she always managed to get him to laugh. Marie would always know just what to do to lift John's spirits. Although keeping Larry and Gary and Mary Beth and Elaine in line during their younger years proved to be a monumental task, she played the mother role extremely well and managed to shed many a light into the cracks and crevices her children sustained when things didn't go as well as they had expected.

And when you look at the West Seneca Garden Club, the Buffalo Fire Department Women's Auxiliary of which she was a member; you'd find that Marie carried out her life's work at each and every one of their gatherings. She'd lift many a person's spirit and shine more than a few rays of sun into the cracks and crevices that may have marred some member's life, all of which can be attested to by boxes filled with letters of thanks from those who benefited by her warmth and her care and her consolation.

So all in all, it could well be said that Marie did as George Papaderos had done; she reflected the sun wherever she went and provided rays of sunshine for many who led a sun starved life.

I am reminded here of a story the late John F. Kennedy Junior once told. He was interviewing the Dalai Lama for his magazine, *George*. On seeing Kennedy's bandaged hand, the Dalai Lama held that hand in both of his and did his best to soothe the wound. When the interview ended and the Dalai Lama and his entourage headed for the door, Kennedy described watching them until they were out of his sight. "I then felt oddly deflated," he said, "it was as if we were all in a dark room and the person with the lantern had just left."

I believe we can say that Marie's death has left many of us feeling as did Kennedy that day. It left us feeling as though we were all in a dark room and the person with the lantern had just left. We can take heart in the fact that if we made it a point to be as positive as was Marie; that if we made it a point to be sweeter and kinder and more joy filled; that if we made it a point to cheer up and uplift those living a sun starved life; if we made it a point to shine the sun's rays into the cracks and crevices that had marred someone's life; then Marie will return with the lantern as she'd be seen living on in us.

And there's also the consolation of knowing that Marie is living on in the resurrected life. Christ came to let us know that when we die, life is changed not ended and when the body of our earthly dwelling lies in death, we gain an everlasting dwelling place in heaven. Marie is now in God's celestial kingdom where pain and suffering is no more. She's back together again with her beloved John and daughter Linda and a good many others whom she loved and who preceded her in death. The good news is that we will see her again.

DEATH BY SUICIDE

Tell of what can be done to soften the tragic loss of someone whose death can't be explained.

Giacomo Puccini, the great Italian composer, has composed such masterpieces as *Madame Butterfly* and *La Boheme*. His most accomplished piece, his masterwork Turandot never got completed. He was diagnosed with cancer shortly after beginning the composition and as his body weakened, he realized that he would not have the time to finish what he started. So before he breathed his last, he gathered his friends together and told them: "Look, it's going to be up to you to finish my Opera!"

When Puccini died, his friends were filled with immense grief. They wished he'd have lived a whole lot longer and they were angry and frustrated because their wish had not come true. They were now faced with the task of burying their dear friend.

Some weeks after the funeral, they recalled Puccini's charge to finish his opera and so they began the process of honoring Puccini's last request. In October of 1926 at the famed La Scala Opera House in Milan, Puccini's final Opera, the one he didn't have time to finish, was to be performed for the first time with none other than the famous Toscanini as the lead conductor. The music began in all of its glory. Fifty minutes later, the music came to an abrupt halt. Toscanini turned around to the audience and announced, with tears running down his face, that they had come to the point where Puccini's work had ended.

After a long pause, he lifted up his head, smiled broadly and said: "And this is where his friends began." From that point forward, there came unbelievably beautiful music that resonated with the tones and the melodies similar to those of the great Puccini.

As all of you know, Mary Smith died this past Sunday. We don't know why she did what she did. We can't fathom a young woman known for her smile and known for lighting up a room; we can't fathom her ending her life when that life had so much promise and potential, when that life was such a blessing to so many.

Early on Sunday, something so overwhelmed her, some powerful thoughts invaded her mind and logic and good sense and the memory of people who loved her could not weaken its power. We are bewildered, grief stricken, and angered that we never saw or realized the depths of Mary's pain. We so wish that we could have done something but, alas, we could not.

What we need to do is what Puccini's friends did. We need to pick ourselves up from our grief and make sure that the Opera of Mary's life gets completed. We need to make sure that the song she sang and the music that resonated throughout her life, we need to make sure it doesn't get buried with her remains.

That means that every one of us is going to have to smile more and be kind more often; that means we're going to have to live more unselfishly and be more considerate of others; that means we're going to have to lift people's spirits and soothe people's pain. If we do those sorts of things, Mary's Opera will get completed, Mary song, the melody of her life will continue on.

Mary Smith will indeed be missed, but the good news is that she's not really gone. We believe as a Christian people that when someone we love dies, that life is changed not ended, that when the body of our earthly dwelling lies in death, we gain an everlasting dwelling place in heaven. Mary may not be physically present anymore, but she lives on in God's celestial kingdom, she lives on in the world beyond this one, a world free of the pain and the suffering and the anguish that overwhelmed her in those final moments of her life.

A TRAGIC DEATH

We gather here in grief and pain because someone we loved has died, and the circumstances of her death and the fact that she died at 21 years of age makes the grief and pain that much more intense and that much more difficult to bear. We wish things could be different, but we know that they can't. We wish we could've done something but there really wasn't anything we could have done. So here we stand lost and bewildered and helpless.

If there's one thing that could be of help, it's our faith, our faith can be our consolation and strength, our faith can be the crutch to get us through our grief, and our faith can be the balm to ease our pain.

That's because, first and foremost, our faith tells us that God is always nearby. When William Sloane Coffin learned his son had died, that his son lost his life when his car veered off the road and plummeted into the Boston River. Someone made the mistake of telling him that it must have been God's will. Coffin flew into a rage. He said it was not God's will that there were no guard rails on that stretch of the highway. It was not God's will that he never got that windshield wiper fixed. It was not God's will that he might've had a few beers too many. "It's my contention and it's my belief," said Coffin, "that when the last wave overtook my son and he breathed his last, the first heart to break and the first tear that was shed was that of God."

I can't help but recall that famed "Footprints in the Sand" story where a man is looking over his life and sees that throughout the journey there were two sets of footprints, his and God's. But he complained to God about the fact that in the most difficult times of life there was but one set of footprints. "Why God, did you abandon me at those times?" And God responded: "I didn't abandon you. There was only one set of footprints because during those times I was carrying you."

118

God is near to all of us. God shares our grief and God shares our sorrow and God shares our pain and probably now God's holding us in his arms. God is closer to us now than God's ever been before, and with God's help, we can endure.

Our faith also tells us that Mary Smith is in God's company, that Mary Smith is in God's celestial home, and as such, Mary isn't really gone. C.S. Lewis lost his friend Charles Williams, and he wrote something that he could've never written before because he'd have considered it sentimental claptrap. He wrote that since Charles Williams died, heaven was no longer a strange and far off place. It had been that once, but now it was a dear and familiar place because his friend Charles Williams was there. Our faith tells us that not only does Mary live on in God's celestial kingdom, but our faith also tells us that heaven is no longer a strange and far off place for any of us, because our friend Mary Smith is there.

And finally, our faith also tells us that there is something we can do in response to Mary's tragic death and that is to make sure that Mary's story doesn't end here. The best memorial we can ever erect, the best tribute we can ever pay Mary is to live our lives more beautifully and more wonderfully, thanks to the impact that life had made upon us. In her brief years of life, Mary had shown us many wonderful qualities.

If we can incorporate those qualities into our own life, then we will make sure that Mary will live on, not just in God's celestial kingdom, but will live on through you and I. My friends, we are a people of faith. Tap into that faith, feel the presence of God, and with God at your side, navigate the waters of grief till that time when peace of mind and heart can finally be attained.

JOHNNY APPLESEED

Tell of their legacy; tell of their unselfish work and its long-lasting benefits.

In Indiana some years back, they erected a statue of a man named John Chapman. He lived in the early part of the 19th century when the Middle Western States (Ohio, Indiana, Michigan, and Illinois) were just getting settled. If you were to consider the outward features of John Chapman's life, you'd be hard-pressed to find anything extraordinary. As a matter of fact, you'd wonder why he would be deserving of a statue erected in his honor. He was what was then called a drifter. He had no regular home. He had no regular job. He hardly ever made a dollar in his life.

For 30 or 40 years, he journeyed continuously over the whole of those four Midwestern States, rarely stopping in one place longer than an overnight stay. Many considered him a bit off, a little strange, perhaps unbalanced because all he ever did was to go from place to place with this sack of apple seeds. He'd either plant those seeds himself or he'd give them to farmers to plant. His one great passion in life was to have those four Midwestern States dotted with apple orchards so the next generation would be able to enjoy the fruit of his labors for many long years to come. John Chapman became known as Johnny Appleseed.

When you think of it, that statue they erected as a memorial to honor John and his work wasn't really necessary. The real memorial was already in existence. It could be found amidst the millions of apple blossoms that dotted the landscape each spring. It could be found in the delicious fruits of those countless orchards which wouldn't be there today if not for him.

If you were to look at the outward features of John Miller's life, they would not appear to be very impressive. After all, he did not hold any prestigious office and didn't have a job that commanded a huge salary. And you'd be hard-pressed to find anything extraordinary when it came to the profession he chose to pursue.

But if we were to review the impact he had upon those who knew him, if you were to gauge the effect he had upon the countless numbers of people whose path crossed his, you'd be astounded. You'd be advocating for a statue to be built in his honor.

So, when all is said and done, John Miller lived an extraordinary life and along the way of that life he sowed many a seed and, thanks to that labor, we find many a life in bloom and many a place array with blossoms thank to his influence, thanks to the effect he had upon them. So, there will be no need to erect a statue in his honor, for a memorial is already in existence in those people and in those places who were lucky enough to have been the beneficiary and recipient of his goodness and devotion and love.

So, we thank God today for the gift of his life and thank God as well that his life is not over, that he lives on in the resurrected life that Jesus promised. We believe that when death comes, life is changed not ended, that when the body of our earthly dwelling lies in death, we gain an everlasting dwelling place in heaven.

ADDITIONAL ILLUSTRATIONS

LONESTAR

There is a popular song by the country-western group Lonestar. It's entitled: *I'm Already There*. It centers around someone in a lonely cold hotel room who misses his family. He calls home and when he hears his kids laughing in the background, tears come to his eyes. A little voice then comes on the phone asking as to when he was coming home and it's then that we hear the song's beautiful refrain.

"I'm already there. Take a look around. I'm the sunshine in your hair. I'm the shadow on the ground. I'm the beat in your heart. I'm the moonlight coming down. I'm the whisper in the wind."

That man in that lonely cold hotel room lets it be known to those he loves that although he is miles away, he's still there in their midst. All they need do is take a look around.

John Smith is not miles away. He is a world away. He's in the place of which the Holy Spirit said: "Eye has not seen, nor ear heard, nor has it entered the hearts of people to know what the Lord has prepared for those who have loved him." That may well be so, but John is still with us. All we need to do is take a look around.

Be at the moonlight coming down, be it the whisper in the wind, be it the beat in our heart, be it at any of those places John Smith happened to frequent, be it a group of his old friends, he is there and will always be there and there will come a time when we'll see him face-to-face in God's eternal home.

DALAI LAMA

Years ago, the late John F. Kennedy Jr. interviewed the Dali Lama for his magazine *George*. Seeing Kennedy's bandaged hand, the Dalai Lama held it in both of his own hands rubbing and patting it. After the Dalai Lama and his entourage had left, Kennedy described watching them until they were out of his sight. "I then felt oddly deflated," he said, "it was as if we were all in a dark room and the person with the lantern had just left."

Mary Smith's death has left us all feeling as Kennedy did that day, it left us feeling as though we were all in a dark room and the person with the lantern had just left. But we can take heart in the fact that if emulate the virtues Mary possessed, if we make it a point to carry on her good works, Mary will return with that lantern because she'll be seen living on in us.

JESUS, IT'S JIMMY

George Macleod was the founder of the Iona community in Scotland. In one of his broadcasts, he concluded with a story about a young man who entered a Catholic Cathedral each day at noon to say a prayer. He would come in, kneel at the altar rail for a few moments and then slip away. The pastor watched this action for several days and then one day stopped the young man and said: "Son, I see you coming each day, but you only stay for a minute. What do you do?" "Oh!" said the young man, "I work down the street. I can only come here during my lunch hour and the time is so short that I only have time for a brief prayer." "What prayer do you say?" asked the priest. The young man responded: "I pray: 'Jesus, it's Jimmy!' and then I leave."

Several months later, the pastor got called to the home of a young man who lay dying. It happened to be the same young man he'd seen every day at noon at the Cathedral. The pastor said that while he was in the room, he had the strange sensation that there was another presence not visible to the eye. As the young man was about to breathe his last breath, the pastor claimed he heard a voice that said: "Jimmy, it's Jesus!"

As you know, Mary Smith was a woman of tremendous faith and she prayed so darn much that I am sure she had a relationship with Jesus, not unlike the one that Jimmy had with the Lord. When Mary Smith died a few days back, I would guess that if you had been there and listened real close, you may well have heard just before she died, a voice that said: "Mary, it's Jesus!"

BRAC STONE

The stone in the doorway to the United Nations building in New York City comes from the Adriatic Island of Brac. So does the stone in the White House in Washington DC. So does the stone that forms the altar of the Liverpool Cathedral in England. So does the stone that forms the church of Sacre Coeur in Paris. The Brac stone is famous all over the world. It can be said that there is a bit of the island of Brac in many, many places.

John Smith may not have been famous all over the world, but it can be said that there's a bit of him in many, many places and a bit of him in many, many lives and that includes your life as well as mine. We thank God today for the gift of John's life and give thanks for the privilege of having his life touch ours.

HAPPY BIRTHDAY

Clarence Jordan, the famed biblical scholar, left detailed instructions for how his funeral service was to be conducted. His final request was to be buried simply in a pine coffin at a particular spot on the farm where he lived and which he loved dearly. One issue he had not addressed was what should be said at the gravesite.

When he died, the funeral service unfolded just as he had planned, and when the community gathered around the designated grave, an awkward silence settled over the crowd. Jordan had always been the one to offer leadership in such a situation, but he was gone. A three-year-old girl who loved Jordan very much must have recognized the awkwardness of that poignant moment and, quite spontaneously, she stepped up to the coffin and began to sing her favorite song: "Happy Birthday." Jordan's biographers observed that there could not have been a more appropriate ending to a remarkable Christian life.

Now I am not suggesting that we all sing Happy Birthday to John Smith, but it would be an appropriate thing to do. John's earthly life is over, and his heavenly life has begun. John has left the womb of this life, only to begin life again. This past Tuesday was John's birthday into new life. So, to you John, I say Happy Birthday! And to those of you John has left behind, I say mourn because you must, but be of good cheer; you were a witness to a wonderful and beautiful and remarkable life.

WINSTON CHURCHILL

At Winston Churchill's funeral, there was a moment when the coffin was to be carried out of Westminster Abbey and onto a barge for a trip down the famed Thames River. A special group of pallbearers from the various military services was selected to assume that task. As it happened, one of the pallbearers, a sailor, broke his ankle as the coffin got carried down the steps of the Abbey. For a moment, it seemed that Churchill's remains would drop to the ground, but it didn't. Instead, it was safely carried onto the barge.

Afterwards, officials inquired of the sailor: "How did you manage to go on with your duty with your ankle broken in two places?" The sailor responded: "I know the caliber of the man I was carrying. And knowing that, even with a broken ankle, I'd have continued to carry him throughout the streets of London."

John Smith was not as famous as Winston Churchill, but I believe he led a life that commanded as much respect and honor, as did he. If a sailor had broken his ankle carrying John Smith to his grave, he'd have gotten him there, nonetheless. And if they asked him how he did it, he'd have said: "I know the caliber of the man I was carrying. Even with a broken ankle, I'd have carried John Smith throughout the streets of Buffalo."

ALICE IN WONDERLAND

I would like to close with a quote from the children's story: *Alice in Wonderland*. It came from a conversation the White Queen is having with Alice. They're talking about memories and the

White Queen, surprised that Alice remembers only things that have already happened, declares: "You know, Alice, it's a poor sort of memory that only thinks backwards."

There is no question we have a lot of good and great memories of John Smith. The best tribute we can pay to John, the best Memorial we could ever build in his honor, is to incorporate into our life the wonderful qualities of living we had seen in his. In that way, we will make new memories of John Smith because people will see John living on through us.

W.H. AUDEN

I close with something the Irish poet W. H. Auden said at the graveside of his friend William Butler Yeats on the day of his burial. He said: "Earth, we give to you an honored guest." We say today: "Lord God, we give to you an honored guest, John Smith. We thank you for the privilege of calling him our friend."

SHIPS IN A HARBOR

Two ships sailed in a harbor. One going out on a voyage and the other coming into port. People cheered the ship going out while the ship sailing in was hardly noticed. Seeing this, a wise man remarked that they had it all wrong. People should be cheering the ship coming in because it reached the shore and it's gotten its passengers safely home. We rejoice today because Mary's ship reached the shores of heaven and she's now safely home. To you Mary, we say goodbye and we also say thank you for having led such a wonderful life

CONTRASTING TOMBSTONES

There are two contrasting tombstones in an old Civil War graveyard. One was a large imposing marker of a deceased general which listed all his battles and accomplishments. The other was a small stone marking the grave of a young woman who died at the age of 21. Her husband's inscription read simply: "Everywhere she went, she brought flowers."

When you think of all the joy and happiness that Mary brought to all of us, I believe it could be said of her that "everywhere she went, she brought flowers."

SAVING PRIVATE RYAN

In Steven Spielberg's movie: *Saving Private Ryan*, a squadron of young soldiers are sent on a mission to find one soldier behind enemy lines and bring him safely home. Most of the young men in the squadron, including the captain, die in the rescue attempt. As he lies dying, the captain's last words to that one soldier Private Ryan are: "Earn This!"

Many years later, Private Ryan, now an old man, visits the grave of that Captain. As he kneels at the grave, he says: "Not a day goes by that I don't think about what happened. I just want you to know I've tried, tried to live my life the best I could. I only hope in your eyes, at least, I earned what you did for me."

My friends, the best tribute you can pay to Mary Smith is to live your life in such a way they it can be said without question that you earned what Mary Smith did for you. That the sacrifices she made, the example she provided, the blessings she bestowed upon you; that you are an exemplary person because of it, that the way you are conducting your life today is a direct result of it. So, when it comes to seeing Mary Smith again, all one has to do is to look at you.

So, make sure, my friends, that what they see will do Mary Smith proud. Make sure that when she looks down upon you from the halls of heaven, she'll smile because she'll know that you earned what she did for you.

MUIR WOODS

In the Muir Woods of California, a phenomenon takes place at times involving one of those giant redwood trees. When a tree of that immense stature gets logged, blown over or destroyed by fire; in other words, when one of those trees dies, the seeds which the tree produced for years, those seeds miraculously begin to sprout all around the place where the giant tree once stood.

Forest Rangers say there are three reasons for its occurrence. The trauma of the tree's death stimulates growth hormones within the seeds. They're also able to absorb the sunlight which was previously blocked by the enormity of the fallen tree; and third, they get moisture and nutrients from the tree's root system which still remains intact even though the tree is gone.

I believe you could say that Mary's children and grandchildren are the seeds that Mary has left behind. And just as she has entered into new life thanks to the resurrection of our Lord Jesus Christ, so are they brought into new life, a life without her company and a life without her presence, love, and tenderness. But thanks to what Mary was to all of them, thanks to the treasured memories which they'll always be able to recall and cherish, they have sunlight, and they have the moisture and the nutrients necessary to help their new life along. Mary Smith may be gone, but she'll forever remained rooted in the lives of those she loved.

BUILDING A CATHEDRAL

I've always liked that story of a traveler from Italy who came to the French town of Chartres to see the cathedral that was in the process of getting built. Arriving at the end of the day, he came to the site just as the workers were preparing to leave the premises. He asked one man, covered with dust, he asked him what he did. The man replied that he was a stonemason. He spent his days carving stones. Another man, when asked, said he was a glassblower, that he spent his days making colored glass. The traveler from Italy asked still another person what he did, and he said he was a blacksmith who pounded iron for a living.

Wandering deep into the worksite of the unfinished Cathedral, the traveler came upon an older woman armed with a broom. She was sweeping the stone chips and the wooden shavings and the glass chards from the day's work. He asked her what she did. She paused, leaned on her broom and looking up toward the high arches that had been set in place, she said: "Me? I'm building a Cathedral for the honor and the glory of Almighty God.

If you asked John Smith as to what he did for a living, he could have given us many different answers. He could've said an optician, a master builder, a car mechanic, you name it. But looking at the family he built and how proud he was of the way they lived their lives, he may well have shared the sentiment of that sweeper of stone chips and wooden shavings and glass chards. If asked as to what he did for a living, he may well have said that he spent his life building human cathedrals for the honor and glory of God.

===

Being the chair of the hospital board, being an educator running a school, being a mother superior may not, in the bigger picture seem like a lot but I think it could be said that in all actuality she was building cathedrals, human cathedrals because so many of the lives she touched in the schools she taught in, and the hospitals she worked in, and the convents where she lived; many of those lives are shining brightly today, many of those lives have become beacons of God's grace, many of those lives are an asset to our society thanks in no small measure to the impact Mary Smith had upon them. They've become human cathedrals for the greater honor and glory of God. How fortunate this world is to have had such a builder, and how fortunate it's been for this community to have had in its midst a builder as great as she.

NAUPAKA FLOWER

In Hawaii, there is a famous legend concerning a peculiar Hawaiian flower called the naupaka. It's peculiar in that it blooms with only a half a blossom. Legend has it that two Hawaiian lovers were separated and forced to live apart. The man was forced to live in the mountains. The woman was forced to live by the sea. Upon learning of their impending separation, the woman took a full naupaka flower. She tore it in half and put one half behind her ear and the other half behind her lover's ear. The story goes that ever since that time, the naupaka blooms in only half blossoms, with one of the halves blooming on the flowers at the top of the mountain, while the other half blooms on the flowers that grow near the sea.

Not only can we be consoled by our faith, a faith that has John Smith living in the greater life beyond this one, but we can also be consoled by the fact that he's back together again with his beloved wife Mary whom he had loved so very much and to whom he was married for over 61 years. It was no secret that John missed Mary terribly. He wasn't the same after she passed on. You could say that the flowers in his life went to half bloom on the day that she died. They are at full bloom now. The two separated lovers are separated no more.

EDWARD THE CONFESSOR

There was both a king and a saint named Edward the Confessor. This Edward was many things, and he was certainly a builder. Almost a thousand years ago, he was responsible for the first Westminster Abbey, a church of chiseled stone and carved wood and painted glass such as England had never seen before. Throughout 15 years, the King watched the Abbey being built. Gradually his strength declined, and the veil separating him from the next life grew thinner and thinner. At last, the end came, and he spoke his final words. "Weep not!" he said. "I go from the land of the dead to the land of the living."

I daresay that Mary would like to place her hand on our shoulders today and say to each of us: "Weep not! I go from the land of the dead to the land of the living. Be of good cheer, for my life may have changed but it has not ended."

EASIER TO BE GOOD

In a cemetery, a little white stone marks the grave of a little girl and on that stoneware were chiseled these words: "A child of whom her playmates said: 'it was easier to be good when she was with us.'"

When you think of how Mary seemed to bring out the best in all of us, when you think of how Mary exemplified unconditional love, I believe it could well be said that "it was easier to be good when Mary was with us."

LAUGHTER IN HEAVEN

I've been told that there's been a debate going on in theological circles ever since the beginning of time. The debate is over the issue of whether there is laughter in heaven. One school of thought says there is no laughter because the whole point of heaven is the serene contemplation of the truth and beauty of God. The other school of thought says that there must be laughter in heaven because God wouldn't have it any other way.

The way I see it, theologians can debate that question all they want. I know for a fact that there is laughter in heaven. I know it because John Smith is there and being there you can bet that there'll be laughter resounding throughout its hallowed walls.

I'LL SING, NOT CRY

A few years back, a movie entitled *I'll Sing, Not Cry* made it to local theatres. It was based upon the book *African Manhunt* which told of the experiences of Pastor Ngonga in Angola, Africa. The most poignant part of the film came when Pastor Ngonga's wife had died. The mourners, many of whom were pagan, gathered in the church to express their grief. Pagans and Christians alike joined together wailing, shrieking, crying out in pain at the death of this beloved woman.

When the Pastor arrived at the church and heard all the mourning, groaning and crying, he stood beside the coffin, raised his hands, and cried out loudly: "Stop all this yelling and howling and crying! This woman was a child of God. She has gone home to her father. Today, we are not crying. We are singing. We are rejoicing."

I couldn't help but think of that scene as I thought of Mary Smith's life. Mary had a penchant for partying and having fun and she always wore a smile. My guess is that if she stood where I'm standing right now, and she saw you carrying on in grief, as you should, she'd be like that Pastor and yell: "Stop that crying, stop that wailing. I've lived a full and happy life and there's nothing to cry or wail about. Sing and Rejoice! Or as Mary would say: "Party On!"

SCRIPTURE INDEX

SCRIPTURE INDEX

www.ingramcontent.com/pod-product-compliance
Lightning Source LLC
Chambersburg PA
CBHW022026090426
42739CB00006BA/301